Earth School 101

Who we are, where we are and why we are here...

Alan Arcieri

Outskirts Press, Inc.
Denver, Colorado

Foreword

"This marvelous book, and the mysteries it explains, will resonate with the deepest stirrings and queries of your soul. It is one of the best, most enlightening books I have ever read. It addresses, answers and explains what your soul has always been seeking.

It has been my great pleasure to have had Alan Arcieri as a guest on my radio show on many occasions. A gifted medium, Alan always succeeds in thrilling, as well as emotionally touching the audience. He imparts high teachings of metaphysics and spiritual wisdom in a nuts-and-bolts way that may be appreciated and used by anyone as a roadmap. The teachings in this book are presented in the most informative and easy-to-understand manner. It is truly destined to become a metaphysical classic."

~**Joyce Keller**, author of *Seven Steps to Heaven, Calling All Angels, Complete Book of Numerology* and *Why God?* and Psychic Radio Host, www.JoyceKeller.com

This book is dedicated to Diana my beloved wife and best friend for her love, support, encouragement and trust.

Acknowledgements

For the love, generosity and support I received from family and friends, it is with heartfelt gratitude that I thank all who made this book possible. Special thanks to all who have given me the privilege to communicate with their loved ones in spirit and generously allowing me to share their experiences and stories.

Many people have been essential to the writing of this book.

I am deeply thankful to Michelle Gellman my spiritual teacher, mentor, and friend, for starting Diana and me on the path to awakening. Your love, wisdom and encouragement changed our lives forever.

To Peggy Lince, for devoting countless hours helping me review, edit and shape volumes of information from the original manuscript. Your meticulous attention to detail, organization and input were invaluable in bringing this book to life. You are truly amazing.

To Beverly Miller, for generously spending many hours of your time, and energy painstakingly reviewing, editing and transforming the book throughout the many stages of its development, adding the immeasurable benefit of your own writing experience. Your contributions, guidance and advice brought the book to a higher level.

A special thanks to Marilyn Weishaar, a wonderful and talented editor who transformed the manuscript, gave shape to my words; smoothing the structure, easing the flow, making the book a much easier read.

To Danny Arcieri, my multitalented brother, for giving me insightful and helpful advice about writing, structure and the cover design.

To Alicia Merlob, my daughter (the genius) and personal assistant for your love, support, contributions and invaluable feedback.

To Bill Steedle, a talented artist, and Christian Arcieri (little Buddha) my nephew, for the fantastic cover photo.

To Robert Pursell special thanks for my picture.

To Brenda Alexander and Joann Puleo, for donating your time, providing valuable input, advice and for supporting this book from the very beginning.

To Ana Alicea wonderful mother-in-law for always making sure all my needs were met. You are an angel.

To Shadow and Kachina, my puppies, for keeping me company till the wee hours of the morning and for never failing to remind me when to take a break.

And most importantly, I want to express my love and gratitude to my first and finest teachers, Peter and Eleanor Arcieri for teaching me the meaning of unconditional love. Better parents no one could ask for.

Special thanks to all the Spirits who work with me from the other side, and to all the departed souls who let me give them a voice.

Introduction

There are many ways to define our fragile existence and many ways to give it meaning. Most importantly it is spirituality that shapes its purpose and gives it perspective. This book is a collection of powerful and profound life-enhancing knowledge and wisdom I acquired as a medium on the spiritual path for the past twenty-eight years. It is a practical guide to healing old wounds and developing higher levels of awareness; to discovering how to look at the world without judgment, fear, guilt, anger or resentment; to understanding why there is good and evil, success and failure, pleasure and pain. It is a way to learn why changing the way you see the world is much better than trying to change the world.

Earth School 101 will take you a quantum leap forward in understanding who you are and why you are here. You will discover hidden spiritual powers, abilities and learn how to use them to make better choices and decisions.

You don't need to join an organization, a club, or go anywhere to experience a deep connection with the Divine Presence, the Creator, One, I AM, Universal Consciousness, Great Spirit, The Light or whatever you want to call God. All you need is an open mind and a desire to grow and unfold spiritually into a life of meaning, purpose, joy, and service. This is a journey to personal enlightenment and empowerment on the path to awakening.

My initial spiritual experiences had a profound effect on me as a child and led me to discover my calling as a Spiritual Medium.

Altar Boy

I went to St. Joseph's Catholic school as a child. Being surrounded by nuns and priests for the first time in my life was quite an experience. I looked up to them as if they were the gatekeepers at Heaven's door. It wasn't long before I discovered if you made them angry, they would show you the gates to hell; I quickly focused on never making them angry.

I was always drawn to the spirituality and eagerly volunteered to serve as an altar boy when asked by one of the priests. The first Mass I served was at 6 a.m. I felt very much at home on the altar; a sense of familiarity surrounded me. I knew deep inside I was experiencing something very special.

The most wonderful thing was that when Mass was over, I could not feel my feet touching the ground as the priest and I walked from the church to the rectory. I was "walking on air"! There was a powerful force of energy radiating from within me and although I knew I was walking, it actually felt like I was floating. It was absolutely amazing! I was lighter than air, walking on a cloud. Intuitively I knew I was being guided to follow the spiritual path. I will never forget that magical experience as long as I live.

About the same time I became an altar boy, my father introduced me to the hobby of coin collecting. I fell in love with it immediately and thus began years of treasure hunting by rummaging through my family and friends' pocket change searching for rare coins.

The Coin

On the way to the beach one Sunday with my family, I spent my time dreaming of finding a gold doubloon from Davy Jones locker washed up on the seashore. In my mind I could see the glimmering coin clearly laying in the sand waiting for me to discover. Being a 12 year old coin collector with a vivid imagination, I had visions of sunken pirate treasure washing up on the beach.

The drive to Jones Beach on the south shore of Long Island took about an hour. I sat in the back of the station wagon silently repeating the prayers I learned at Catholic school. It was a stream of "Our Father's" and "Hail Mary's" one after another.

My mother was concerned that something was wrong because I was so quiet. She asked if I was alright.

I told her I was fine and resumed my prayers. I prayed like never prayed before, asking God to help me find a coin on the beach that day.

After helping my mother spread out a large red beach blanket and get settled, I took off my sneakers and ran to the shoreline as fast as I could. With my feet in the cool, lapping seawater I continued praying. I walked slowly with my head bowed looking for a coin sticking out of the hard, wet sand leading down the vacant shoreline.

A steady breeze was blowing off the ocean, with the sun breaking through the clouds every now and then, lighting up the overcast sky. For a few moments I completely forgot about the coin; I was totally lost in prayer.

After walking a short distance, I stopped and looked out over the Atlantic's vast horizon. The breeze had turned into a strong wind sending large waves crashing wildly on the beach. My attention was drawn to one giant wave that came ashore with a thundering roar. Out of the corner of my eye, I saw a small dark object rolling out of the wave about fifteen or twenty feet to my right. I was mesmerized by this tiny black object as it rolled out of the ocean, through the crashing waves, over the smooth wet sand right toward me as if being guided by an invisible hand. It landed squarely right between my bare feet. I stared at it for a few seconds, not knowing what to make of it. When I reached down and picked it up I discovered it was an old English coin! My eyes bulged! I was absolutely ecstatic, not about the coin, but about the fact that _someone was listening_... *That God had heard my prayers!* I yelled up to heaven as loud as I could. "Thank you! Thank you! *Thank you!*"

Examining the coin closely, (which was not from Davy Jones Locker) I noticed it was tarnished black on one side and shiny silver on the other. It was as if on one hand the coin was in the ocean for many years and on the other hand for only a matter of minutes. I couldn't believe my eyes!

From that day forward, I realized — *I knew* — we are not alone; that a benevolent, invisible spiritual power we call God is watching over us and *that prayers could be answered.*

This experience compelled me to start on the spiritual path. I had have gone over the events of that day thousands of times trying to figure out exactly what happened and how I made that powerful connection with God. I wanted to know more. I wanted to do more. I wanted to be more. Every time I began to doubt the existence of God and the spirit world, I remembered the coin. That half tarnished, half clean, old English Six Pence came to represent the two paths in life, the dark side and the Light. I spent the next twenty years trying to get back *on the beach* spiritually.

I yearned to re-establish the direct line of communication with God that I experienced on the beach. What exactly did I do? How did I do it? Was it the prayers? Was it me? What did I have to do to communicate with the spirit world? The answers eluded me for many years.

Before discovering the correct path to take, I was shown all the wrong ones. I got lost for a while as a young man and found myself walking down a dark path with more questions than answers. It was a time of confusion and chaos. I lost my identity. I lost my power. I lost my way. I sought comfort in alcohol and drugs. I searched in vain trying to find myself. Who am I? Where am I? Why am I here? Everywhere I looked I was surrounded by darkness, fear and guilt. Deep inside my soul I knew something of great value was missing. I was disappointed in the watered-down spirituality of the church. I was disappointed in the violent, superficial, materialistic world and I was disappointed in myself. In the darkness I realized it was time for a change and the only thing I had the power to change was myself.

Whenever I found myself questioning the existence of God, I remembered the old English coin I found that day on the beach. I knew that if God was listening then, He was listening now. That one profound experience was my guiding light in the deep dark woods.

Then an incredible thing happened to me in 1981. It changed my life forever. As the saying goes, when the student is ready a teacher appears. My spiritual mentor, guide, teacher and friend Michelle Gellman appeared and my life would never be the same. Through newly humbled eyes I was shown amazing things. She introduced me to metaphysics and taught me how to meditate. She showed me the bridge to the spirit world I'd been seeking my entire life. Michelle introduced me to spirituality without employing fear and guilt. I learned we are Divine beings with unlimited potential capable of extraordinary things. I had no idea how extraordinary we really are.

Back on the beach

Shortly after I began meditating daily, spiritual beings with a bright white light behind them approached me. I could see their heads, shoulders arms and bodies clearly, although I could not see their facial features. At first I thought I was hallucinating. I was startled to see them but intuitively I knew there was nothing to fear. The spirits came closer waiting for me to make contact. I discovered I could speak to them telepathically and they would respond to my thoughts. I wasn't able to hear them clearly but they could hear me. They began showing me future events in my life which at the time made no sense. Many years later their messages became abundantly clear.

A short time later my late grandfather and a favorite uncle suddenly appeared side by side in front of me. They were surrounded by a bright white Light. They encouraged me to follow the path I was on and assured me they would provide assistance from the other side. As a feeling of peace and tranquility washed over me they faded away as quickly as they appeared. I was so overcome with joy I wanted to cry and laugh at the same time. I've been on a spiritual quest ever since.

After years of searching, I was on the beach again. This time, instead of coins coming out of the waves, souls were coming out of the spirit world and they wanted to talk to me.

Table of Contents

Foreword
Dedication
Acknowledgments
Introduction
Chapter 1   Earth School 101 1
Chapter 2   Science Meets Spirituality 15
Chapter 3   We are Creators 33
Chapter 4   The New God.. 41
Chapter 5   Trust 55
Chapter 6   The Ego and Higher Self........................... 61
Chapter 7   Reincarnation 67
Chapter 8   Karma 79
Chapter 9   Forgiveness.. 85
Chapter 10 Destiny and Free Will 91
Chapter 11 Time Control... 103
Chapter 12 Negative Energy 109
Chapter 13 Meditation... 123
Chapter 14 Spirit Guides and Guardian Angels 135
Chapter 15 Death.. 145
Chapter 16 Near Death Experiences 155
Chapter 17 Alzheimer's, Dementia and Coma 161

Chapter 18   Suicide 171
Chapter 19   Spirit Communication 179
Chapter 20   Spiritual Protection................................. 195
Chapter 21   Other Dimensions.................................... 199
Frequently Asked Questions 203
Alan's Website

Chapter 1
Earth School 101

We are not humans having a spiritual experience,
we are spirits having a human experience.
~*Teilhard de Chardin*

Have you ever wondered:

- What happens to us when we die?
- Where do we go?
- Why do some people live one hundred years and others one hundred days?
- Why are some born filthy rich and others dirt poor?
- Why do bad things happen to good people?
- Who are we?
- Where are we?
- Why are we here?

The following chapters provide compelling answers to these timeless questions without employing fear, guilt or dogma. See where cutting-edge discoveries in science take spirituality out of the dark ages into the twenty-first century. The only requirements are a desire to learn and an open mind.

It is important to realize that we are not mortal humans having spiritual experiences; we are eternal spiritual beings having human experiences. We are spiritual beings in human form. The spirit world, not the physical world, is our true home. Earth is actually a school our soul visits to learn spiritual lessons. We leave home, go to school, and return home. Life is a gift that offers us the opportunity to learn spiritual lessons.

We come to Earth to learn about love and forgiveness; not only the joy and pleasure of love, but also the pain of love. Love is a diamond with many facets. On Earth we are given the opportunity to learn about the power of love in ways we cannot experience in the spirit world.

We also learn nothing in life is left to chance. Everyone comes into our lives to teach us something or to learn from us; most of the time both. Everyone and everything in life is our teacher.

The chaotic and often painful experiences we encounter are required for our spiritual growth and development. If we ask for patience, we are not given patience; we are given opportunities to be patient. If we ask for strength, we are given opportunities to be strong. If we ask for courage, we are given opportunities to be brave. Before we can save the world, we must first save ourselves. We save ourselves and the world through acts of kindness and compassion. The world is a meaningful place and everything that happens in life happens by design to assist in our self-actualization.

Without the conflicts and challenges in life, everything would be perfect and there would be no growth. How can we develop courage and strength without life's problems and obstacles? By overcoming these challenges we become humbler, more mature souls. We grow and evolve spiritually learning to live with a peaceful heart.

There are no classes to prepare us for life; we are asked to face it head on. Negative experiences — failures and mistakes — are essential elements for our spiritual growth and development. Failure is a priceless form of feedback that holds opportunities to learn and move forward. Learning from negative experiences provides us with rich insights and extraordinary clarity. By overcoming challenges in life we serve as examples and help others find courage, strength, honor and integrity.

Smooth Seas Do Not Make Skillful Sailors

Although we would all like to sail through life with few problems, we would not have a lot to show for those incarnations when we go home. Because it takes a lot of effort and energy to live in the physical world we need to make the most of the time we have here. We need to realize our spiritual powers and abilities and learn to become skillful sailors.

Life's problems and the obstacles are not here to stop us, they are here to help us grow. If the challenges are great enough they will bring out hidden strengths and abilities. We are not in this boat alone. We have an invisible spiritual support team guiding and protecting us along the way. (See Chapter 14, Spirit Guides)

Our spirits are strengthened by working through conflicts and challenges. We can't give up because nothing is over until we stop trying.

The greatest gifts we can show one another are unconditional love, compassion, and forgiveness. By understanding the spiritual aspects of our lives we are able to transform our darkest moments into learning experiences. We can give meaning to the pain we have endured and begin to heal from the inside out. As we realize our true purpose in life, we attain meaning, fulfillment, peace, and the ability to overcome limitations while living in a world full of challenges.

Pain Can Become Power

We are not here to suffer; we are here to learn. We can use every painful situation to grow and gain joy, clarity, and confidence. Being cold makes us appreciate warmth; hunger makes us appreciate having plenty.

Divine Order is behind everything we see as senseless suffering. With experience we can transform that pain into power. Some of life's most enjoyable and rewarding experiences are born from negative experiences. Pain draws us apart from the world and closer to the Creator. Having a health issue for example can put us on a new path in life. I know a man who had his hands and feet amputated after spending the night flat on his back on a frozen lake in subzero weather. He was high on drugs and it was a miracle he survived the ordeal. Against all odds, Daniel R. Davison mastered the use of four artificial limbs, learned to drive, play the drums, ride horses, and sky dive. On top of that, he not only learned to sail, he raced in the American Cup and founded a sailing program for people with handicaps. Today Daniel is an outstanding inspirational speaker who uses his hard-won wisdom inspiring people to let go of limiting beliefs. He is a living testament to the power of the human spirit. His motto is: *"You are Your Choices."*® Daniel is a perfect example of transforming the pain of a life-threatening experience into clarity and confidence. He radiates an immense amount of positive energy now. No one is ever the same after meeting this incredible man. It is an honor and a privilege to know him.

On Earth we learn from negative experiences in a way we cannot learn when we are home. We cannot feel hunger and cold when we are home. We cannot feel separation, fear, anger, worry, pain and despair. Darkness is not part of the spirit world; there is only Light.

We can look at an apple. We can touch it, weigh it and measure it. Only when we eat the apple will we know it completely. On earth we are able to taste the many different flavors that life offers. It is only here in the physical world that we can know them completely, both the sweet and sour. On a higher level these diverse experiences are serving our souls' purpose.

In school you get the lesson and then take the test.
In life you take the test and then get the lesson.
~ Unknown

Alan Arcieri

We Learn from Those Who Challenge Us

The antagonists in our life cause us the most stress and anxiety, yet they are our best teachers. They teach us to have courage, strength, patience, and forgiveness — these things are easy to say and hard to do. They are essential to our spiritual growth and development. Without antagonists we would never have the opportunity to learn these priceless lessons.

These teachers are usually the people closest to us, like family members who know how to push our buttons. They ignite our reactive nature. They raise their voices; we raise ours even higher. They push us and we push back harder. We are here at the Earth school to learn to overcome our reactive nature (aka the ego), our lower self and connect with our higher self. (See Chapter 6, Ego)

Problems cannot be solved on the same level on which they were created. We must rise above the negativity to avoid generating more negative energy or be impacted by it. By doing so we are able to see the situation with more clarity; we are able to see roads to healing which can't be seen on the lower levels.

Imagine being lost in a big city. Tall buildings obscure the view but if we climbed the tallest building we would have a clear view of the city below. We would know exactly where we are and which direction to take to find our way home.

From the higher view it is possible to see future events before they happen and take appropriate action to create a desired outcome. We can see one car speeding down a side street and another car speeding toward it from the other direction and predict the outcome. There is a distinct advantage to being on a higher level. The same thing is true in life. When we raise our consciousness above the negative energy generated on the lower levels, we can see roads to healing and make the appropriate changes in time to avert disaster.

> Life is ten percent what happens to us and ninety percent how we respond to it.
> ~ *Charles Swindoll*

We Are Born with a Life Chart

Before we are born our spirit guides and teachers help us create a life chart containing all of our hopes, dreams, and aspirations. It is designed specifically so that we learn certain spiritual lessons we need during our lifetime. We, along with our teachers and guides, choose the cultures into which we are born, our families, our mothers, fathers, sisters and brothers. We even choose our bodies.

Everyone is in our life by design and has a specific role to play. We have spiritual connections to everyone we meet, especially the antagonists. There are no accidents or coincidences, even though it appears that way. We are responsible for everything in our lives. Even the most unpleasant and chaotic situations are essential for the unique lessons those dynamics provide. This means:

We are not victims, we are volunteers.

Right now you are probably asking, "What was I thinking? Why would I ever volunteer for a life like this? Why wouldn't I choose to be healthy and wealthy with all the benefits of life? Why would I ever want anything less than that?"

Although privileged lifestyles would be our priority on this side, they are not when we are home. Our priorities on Earth are very different than they are in the spirit world. Invaluable opportunities to learn more about ourselves and grow spiritually are sometimes disguised in life as unpleasant events.

Life on Earth Is Spiritual Boot Camp

We come to Earth with all the powers, abilities, and tools we need to help us learn our lessons; without them we would have no reason to be here. These are powerful spiritual tools that help us develop our intuition so we can make better choices and decisions in life.

We return to Earth over and over again to learn these priceless lessons from a wide variety of cultural, religious, and ethnic backgrounds. It may take many lifetimes to learn a lesson, but once we do, we learn it for all eternity. (See Chapter 7, Reincarnation)

The Veil of Forgetfulness

A *veil of forgetfulness* is placed over our consciousness at birth to create the illusion of separation from the spirit world and from our past lives. This veil creates an amnesiac block so we can concentrate on this life without interference from past life memories. Some people have a very thick blanket; they see nothing beyond the material world. Other people have a very thin veil and they can easily connect with the other side.

Spirit communication is possible when we open the veil. Mediums are a bridge between the physical and the spirit worlds. People with Alzheimer's or dementia will often communicate with departed loved ones who come to take them home. Their veil is wide open enabling them to see and hear nonphysical beings. (See Chapter 19, Spirit Communication)

Through hypnosis we can remove the veil and visit past lives. One of my favorite books on this subject is "Many Lives Many Masters" by Dr. Brian Weiss. Past life regression can help us understand why certain people and situations occur in our lives. (See Chapter 8, Karma)

We Are Creators

We are not only the actors in this play of life; we are also the writers and the directors. This life can be heaven or it can be hell; the choice is ours. We create the story-line. If we want to see our best friend, we need only look in the mirror. If we want to see our worst enemy, we need only look in that very same mirror.

The length of life is not important; it is our perform-ance that counts. Don't be afraid to take risks along the way. We must have courage to move beyond our comfort zone and take chances in order to grow. If we stay in one place and play it safe there is no opportunity for growth. When we take action we move from the passenger seat into the driver's seat of our highest destiny. (See Chapter 3, We are Creators)

Fate Is Simply a Future That You Didn't Try to Change

A Divine Order lies behind all the suffering and pain we endure on Earth. Whenever anything painful happens, a priceless lesson is concealed within it. There are many levels and layers to the lessons life teaches.

Because we are unable to see the bigger picture, life appears to be chaos; however bedlam is an illusion due to the lack of vision. We only perceive events as accidents and coincidences because on Earth we can't see far enough. Accidents are our training in life, opportunities for us to learn and grow in wisdom.

On a higher level, everything, even the most horrendous tragedy has a reason for happening. Our lives are like small pieces of a ten-thousand piece jigsaw puzzle. No matter how long we examine this one short lifetime, we will never be able to complete the puzzle. Staring at it will only generate more stress and anxiety because it is impossible to see the big picture.

Chaos appears when we can't see far enough. Trying to figure out why bad things happen to good people is like looking at one small piece of a puzzle. This one life we are living is just one small link in a chain of lifetimes on our soul's journey through eternity. It is not until we return home from school that we will understand where this lifetime fits into a much bigger picture.

Since we are volunteers and not victims, we can't point our finger at anyone and blame them for our problems. We must take *full responsibility* for everything in our lives, especially the most chaotic situations. For example:

Imagine every time we came to the Earth School, we gave up our power to alcohol and became alcoholics. We may choose a lifetime where we are the only sober one in a family to experience alcohol from a new perspective. We are given the opportunity to learn the devastating effects that alcohol abuse has on the family circle. Everywhere we turn there's chaos, pain, suffering, and despair. We get angry and look up to heaven and scream to God, "There must be some mistake! I don't belong here! Everyone is drunk! This is so unfair! Why me?"

We might think that we are being punished, or are a victim of some cruel joke that God is playing on us. The truth is *we chose this dynamic* in order to learn firsthand from a sober perspective how alcohol abuse destroys people. We can't play the victim and blame all of our problems on bad luck, our dysfunctional family, our environment or anyone around us, because _we chose it_. There are no accidents. Everyone is in our life by design playing roles as both students and teachers. We can't change them. We can only change ourselves. We do that the moment we take responsibility for all our situations and circumstances. If we want to know who we were in a past life, we need only to look at who we are now. Who we will be in a future life depends on what we do today.

It is never too late for a new, powerful beginning. The journey to awakening begins today.

> The great thing in this world is
> not so much where we are...but in
> what direction we are moving...
> ~*Oliver Wendell Holmes*

Sometimes we are running through life so fast we not only forget where we have been, but also where we are going. We must get off the fast track to nowhere and savor our journey through life one step at a time. Life today slips through our fingers by living in the past or by worrying about the future. We must plan for tomorrow but live in the present moment. All we really have is this very moment, the Now. This is where we find the doorway to the other side. This is where we are free. Fear of the future and regrets of the past fade away, and are replaced with a deep sense of peace and tranquility. Our spiritual batteries are charged. We become self-empowered; make wiser choices and decisions which benefit us and everyone around us. (See Chapter 13, Meditation)

In the present moment we listen to inner guidance sent to us from the spirit world. We can take many roads between birth and death. The choice is ours. Some roads are long and hard; others are much shorter and smoother. We have to ask ourselves, which road we want to take. Would we rather hack our way through the jungle or fly over it? There is not an easy way out. Life is challenging by design. Some roads are much harder than others. We can't jump from A to Z without going through all the steps in between.

(See Chapter 10, Destiny and Free Will)

Even though we may start life on a long hard road, we don't have to stay there. In the present moment, we access our intuition, our internal guidance system, leading us to the best roads to take on our journey through life. The key to changing our lives is higher awareness. Unfortunately most people live their entire lives in victim consciousness, filled with sorrow, regret, anger, fear and guilt. At death they return home never using the spiritual powers, abilities, and tools with which they were born. It's too late to use those life enhancing tools when we die.

We don't remember what school is all about because the veil of forgetfulness was placed over our consciousness at birth. This book shows how to remove the veil and become self-empowered. We didn't come to the Earth School to be good; we came here to be better. Only the most courageous souls come here to learn.

When we understand the lessons we are being taught through our painful experiences we are able to help other people who are going through the same pain now. We are here to help one another with acts of kindness, compassion and forgiveness. If we help other people in their time of need, someone will be there to help us in ours.

> Kindness is a language which
> the dumb can speak, the deaf
> can understand.
> ~Mark Twain

Spirit is not only found in holy places; it is everywhere and in everything. Every step we take is on holy ground, every breath we take is sacred. This includes our relationships at home and at work. Through the eyes of a child we can see the power and beauty of God in a single blade of grass. Be open to life's wonder and mystery, it is more sacred and meaningful then we are led to believe. Replace fear and regret with unconditional love and forgiveness. The deeper we listen to our soul, the more meaningful life becomes. The answers are within waiting for us to discover.

Laughter is the Music of the Soul

Most importantly we must never lose our sense of humor; it brings us strength beyond measure. Laughter provides insight and tolerance. It is a gift that brings joy and heals the soul. Laughter also reduces stress and strengthens the immune system, releasing chemicals that facilitate healing on all levels. It is the key to sanity.

Groups of people laughing together contribute healing energy to the collective whole. Joy is one of the highest vibrations on this planet. Bring the joy to life by laughing often, especially at yourself. We are not here to see through one another, but to see one another through.

> We don't stop laughing because
> we get old; we get old because
> we stop laughing.
> ~*Michael Pritchard*

Chapter 2
Science Meets Spirituality

Everyone who is seriously involved in the pursuit of science becomes convinced a Spirit is manifest in the Laws of the Universe.

~ Albert Einstein

Human beings live in a world of illusion created by the five senses: sight, sound, smell, taste, and touch. Those senses are limited by a narrow range of reception that locks us into the physical universe. A magician uses the power of illusion to trick us into believing the impossible, such as cutting a person in half and putting him/her back together unharmed. By the same token, our five senses create powerful illusions that fool our perception of reality.

For thousands of years mankind thought the world was flat. This illusion is easy to understand; it appears as though the sun moves and the Earth stands still. Our five senses cannot be trusted to tell us the truth. Over time, science has exposed these visual deceptions as sensory illusions and revealed Earth's true shape and location in the universe.

To add to this dilemma our ancestors were told if they sailed their ship too far out to sea, the ship would fall off the edge of the world. The story was a fear-based false belief that created an imaginary boundary. This feature kept people boxed in, stagnating mankind's growth and development. It wasn't until someone pushed that boundary and discovered the world was round that life on Earth changed forever.

Another illusion is that we are sitting or standing still, not moving at all; in fact, we are traveling through space at half a million miles an hour. At the same time Earth is rotating on its axis at close to a thousand miles an hour. Human beings fail to sense this motion and are under the illusion that Earth is not moving at all.

The sad truth is a little more than five hundred years ago one could have been burned at the stake for saying the world was round, the Earth orbits the sun, or our planet is not the center of the universe. Hundreds, perhaps thousands, of people died for saying things that everyone today — including young school children — know to be true.

Between 1593 and 1600, a monk named Giordano Bruno was locked up in the Papal prison, then burned at the stake as a heretic by the Catholic Church for saying the stars at night are just like our sun, the universe is infinite, and there are other planets with intelligent life.

Time gives all and takes all
away; everything changes but
nothing perishes. There is no
absolute up or down, as Aris-
totle taught; no absolute position in space; but the position
of a body is relative to that of
other bodies. Everywhere
there is incessant relative
change in position throughout
the universe, and the observer
is always at the center of
things.
~*Giordano Bruno*

In 1633, the Catholic Church ordered Galileo, the
father of modern astronomy, to stand trial for heresy.
The sentence of the Inquisition came in three parts:
First, he had to recant his heretical idea the sun was
stationery and that Earth orbited it. Second, he was ordered imprisoned, which was later changed to house arrest for the rest of his life. Third, the publication of any
of his books was forbidden including anything he
would write in the future.

To assert that the Earth revolves around the sun is as erroneous as to claim that Jesus
was not born of a virgin.
~ *Cardinal Bellarmine,
during the trial of Galileo*

Under house arrest, Galileo wrote one of his finest works, "Two New Sciences" (which was published in the Netherlands beyond the Inquisition's reach). Later it was praised by Sir Isaac Newton and Albert Einstein. Because of this groundbreaking book, Galileo is often called the father of modern physics. Galileo died in 1642, still under house arrest.

Church doctrine included a flat Earth was at the center of the universe around which everything revolved. At that time, Rome was the center of power on Earth putting the Catholic Church in the *center of the universe*. Church leaders did not want to give up this lofty position of being "Rulers of the Universe." The Church's real enemy was the printing press because books contained scientific information which challenged the Pope's authority.

Information and education triggered the Spanish Inquisition. Book burning, murder, and torture were wholesale — all in the name of Christ. The Dominicans, who were in charge of the churches' torture chambers during the Inquisition, had their crucifixes covered with a black veil so Jesus wouldn't have to witness what was going on in his name. The Inquisition lasted for more than three hundred years until it was stopped by Napoleon.

It wasn't until 1966 that the Vatican ended its ban on reading certain books. On October 31, 1992, three hundred and fifty years after Galileo's death, the Catholic Church finally admitted it was wrong and apologized.

Galileo and Bruno paid a high price for speaking the truth in the face of myths and superstitions supported by religious authorities who had the agenda of suppressing self-empowering information so they could stay in power.

Ignorance and intolerance generate fear, guilt, and anger. Knowledge and wisdom generate unconditional love, compassion, and forgiveness. Our lack of understanding of the spirit world is in direct proportion to our level of fear, guilt and anger.

> Great spirits have always encountered violent opposition from mediocre minds. The mediocre mind is incapable of understanding the man who refuses to bow blindly to conventional prejudices and chooses instead to express his opinions courageously and honestly.
> ~*Albert Einstein*

Death is the Greatest Illusion

The greatest illusion of all is that life ends at death when, in fact, the soul steps out of the physical body, the same way we step out of a broken-down car. Science has proved that energy can be changed but not destroyed. We are spiritual beings with unlimited potential, temporarily occupying a human body. The physical body dies, but our spirit is immortal. Our heritage is sacred. We are using the human experience as one phase of our soul's evolution. What can be seen with our eyes is temporary. What cannot be seen is *eternal*.

Our spiritual body is pure energy, vibrating at a frequency beyond our range of reception. We can't see radio waves, which are bombarding us all the time, because their energy frequencies are outside our range of reception. We can't hear the higher frequencies of a dog whistle for the same reason. We can't see or hear the spirit world because it vibrates at a frequency beyond our range of reception. Our limited sense of sight, sound, smell, taste, and touch blind us to anything beyond the physical realm. We don't see things as they really are because our human body's range of reception is extremely limited. Just because we can't see or hear the spirit world does not mean it is not all around us.

> The illusion that we are separate
> from one another is an optical delusion of our consciousness.
> ~ *Albert Einstein*

Matter is Energy

Groundbreaking discoveries in quantum physics have brought scientists face to face with the spirit world. For the first time in history, a physicist can sit down with a mystic and, in a matter of minutes, we cannot tell them apart. We are watching science come full circle and merge with spirituality. Scientists and sages agree the paths of science and spirituality lead us to the same fundamental truth: *At the deepest level of reality, we are all One.*

Early in the twentieth century, scientists learned everything we observe as solid matter in the universe is actually made up of particles of energy. At a fundamental level these are subatomic particles called "quarks" and "electrons" which join together to form atoms. Inside the atom, the subatomic particles are traveling around at lightning speed. An atom is so small if one were blown up to the size of a football field, the nucleus in the center would be the size of a grain of sand, and the subatomic particles around the nucleus would be like specs of dust. Less than one percent of the atom can be seen with powerful microscopes, and more than ninety-nine percent appears to be empty space. Atoms gather in a *highly organized arrangement* and become the molecules of rocks, plants, animals, and everything in the physical universe — including humans. Everything and everyone is energy. We live in a vibrating universe where everything is energy from mental thoughts to material things.

> Mass is no longer associated with a material substance. . . . Particles are seen as bundles of energy.
> ~ *F. Capra, physicist*

Everything is made up of particles of energy, from stone to steel, from plants to people. We live in an ocean of energy particles we call the physical universe. There are no exceptions. All matter is energy. No matter how powerful the microscope, we will never find a single particle of matter! Science teaches us energy vibrates at various frequencies. Human beings can see minerals, plants, animals, stars and so on, while radio waves and the earth's electromagnetic field are invisible.

Consider these facts:

- Subatomic energy particles join together to create atoms.
- The atoms join together to create molecules. (If all the information contained in one molecule of DNA were put on paper, it would fill over five thousand pages.)
- No two atoms ever touch each other. (The distance between atoms is like a distance between the Earth and the Sun. Molecules are mostly space.)
- The molecules join together to create cells.
- The cells join together to create the human body.
- There are close to a hundred trillion cells in the average human body. The number of energy particles joined together to form all of the cells in a human body is staggering. Each one of these cells is programmed to perform a particular task. All the cells in the body have to know instantaneously what all the other cells are doing for the human body to function properly. Every particle in our body is connected to every other particle. There is a constant dialogue of information among our heart, brain, and all other organs operating the body. If this dialogue ceases, the body dies.
- When we look in a mirror, we only see one percent of who we are. Our physical body vibrates at a very low frequency and is seen clearly with our eyes. At the same time, ninety-nine percent of who we are is *invisible*

spiritual energy occupying the physical body. This spiritual energy is our *light body*. We are more spirit than flesh.

More food for thought:

- When we eat, do we have to tell the vitamins and minerals where to go?
- Do we have to tell the proteins and the carbohydrates what to do?
- Do we have to tell a cut on our finger how to heal?

Of course not. All these complex processes are handled for us automatically by this highly organized, highly intelligent field of energy and information. All we need to do is eat balanced meals, and everything else is automatically handled for us. Our bodies are programmed to function this way for us by a Higher Intelligence. It is ignorant to think we are in charge of anything. Most of us have a hard time eating balanced meals!

We Are Stardust

DNA is the genetic code for all life on earth. The fundamental building blocks of life found in our DNA are the elements nitrogen, hydrogen, oxygen, and carbon.

These four primordial elements — along with the iron in our blood and the calcium in our bones — came from burned-out stars called "supernovas" which exploded billions of years ago. At this very moment, these fundamental cosmic elements are flowing through our bloodstream. Human beings are literally made of stardust! Life on Earth came from ancient star systems, billions of years older than our solar system. We are literally one with the universe.

When we throw a pebble into a pond, every molecule of water in that pond is affected by the ripple. By the same token, our thoughts and intentions are fields of energy radiating out from us in all directions into the ocean of energy we call the universe. The universe is a seamless fabric of energy of which we are all a part. We are one with the Divine Source of infinite intelligence that created everything from the vastness of the universe to the complex genetic codes in our DNA. Our existence is part of a never-ending creative process which is constantly unfolding. From the vastness of the universe to deep inside the atom, we are a paradox of being both microscopic and macrocosmic. *We are the universe knowing itself.*

> If we could measure the sum total of the number of minds in the universe, there would be just one.
> ~ *Erwin Shrodinger,*
> *quantum physicist*

Apple Seeds

Hidden inside an apple seed are complex genetic codes which will produce a whole new tree filled with apples. Over time, one tiny seed could produce an apple orchard covering the side of a mountain.

Every grade school child knows how to plant a seed. But when we look at what is actually happening within the seed to make it grow, it is nothing short of a miracle. The apple seed is small, dark, and circular. Looking at it through a microscope, we can see the cells. As we look closer, we see each cell is made of molecules. As we look *closer,* we see each molecule is made of atoms. If we look yet closer, we see each atom is made of subatomic particles of "nonphysical energy" whirling at lightning speed. The energy particles bond with each other flawlessly, effortlessly and intelligently to form complex genetic codes to create a new apple tree.

The same thing is true for all life on earth and everything in the universe. Every living thing contains the complex genetic codes necessary to perpetuate the species. It is nothing short of a miracle how energy particles join together in a single microscopic cell to create a human being complete with self-conscious intelligence. When we pay close attention to the world around us, even a simple apple seed can become extraordinarily magnificent and mysterious. Divine Intelligence is constantly working miracles in everything everywhere; yet we take them all for granted.

> If we could see the miracle of a
> single flower clearly, our whole
> life would change.
> ~ *Buddha*

The End of the Dark Ages

Humanity is about to take its next evolutionary step forward in consciousness. One day in the near future mankind will look back at this time in history as *the end of the dark ages*. The "end of days" we thought we were alone in the universe. Cutting-edge discoveries in quantum physics are taking science and spirituality out of the dark ages and into the twenty-first century.

Theoretical physicists have discovered we do not live in a universe. We live in a "Multiverse." Each universe is inside of the other. It is incorrect to think they are on different levels or layers. Each universe/dimension occupies the same space. They do not interfere with each other because of their unique laws of physics. All of the universes are interconnected with each other intrinsically. The question is not if these other universes exist; rather, the question is, "How many universes are there?"

According to "String Theory," theoretical physicists estimate there are ten dimensions. These other universes/dimensions are what the ancient mystics called the spirit world. They are the same exact place, no matter what they are labeled. Ancient Kabbalists taught about the existence of ten dimensions called *Sephirot*. Modern science is validating what our ancestors have known for thousands of years. (See Chapter 21, Other Dimensions)

If we want to know where the spirit world is located, all we have to do is look around us because we are right in the middle of it. The spirit realm coexists with ours. We are "multidimensional" beings coexisting simultaneously in the physical world and in the spirit world. When we die in the physical world, we "wake up" in the spirit world and realize we are home and that we were never away from home to begin with. Separation from the spirit world is just another illusion created by our five senses.

> Behind it all is surely an idea so simple, so beautiful so compelling that when — in a decade, a century, a millennium — we grasp it, we will say to each other, how could it have been otherwise? How can we have been so blind for so long?
> ~John Wheeler,
> theoretical physicist

Time is another Illusion

Physicists and mystics agree, what appears to be empty space is a vast field of energy and information. Albert Einstein's theory of relativity states time is relative to speed, $E=mc2$. Space and time are connected as one unit called Spacetime. Light travels at 186,282 miles a second. The closer we travel to the speed of light the more time slows down.

Time stops at the speed of light. Theoretically, if we were traveling faster than the speed of light, we would travel back in time. Believe it or not, when we look at the stars at night we are actually looking back in time. The light from the most distant stars has traveled for millions of years to reach Earth. Some of those stars shining brightly in the night sky have burned-out millions of years ago. Time is not fixed the way it appears here on Earth.

Time is relative to how fast we are moving. For example:

The Twins Paradox

Twin baby boys are separated at birth. One boy is put in a rocket ship and sent into outer space at eighty percent the speed of light. The other boy remained on earth. On their 60th birthday the rocket ship returns to earth so the twins can celebrate together. The twin who stayed on earth is now a sixty-year-old man. The doors open on the rocket ship and outs steps his twin brother, who is a five-year-old boy. Why? Time in the rocket ship moved slower because it was traveling close to the speed of light. This is not science fiction. Time and space are fragments of eternity. We use time as a unit of measurement on earth and see it as traveling from the past into the future.

In the third dimension we observe time traveling:

1. From the past
2. In the present
3. Into the future.

Time is the measurement of one physical object moving around other physical objects. On Earth one orbit around the sun is a year consisting of three hundred sixty five days. One rotation of the Earth on its axis is a day consisting of twenty-four hours. The units of time on Earth are unique to our planet. A year on Mars is six hundred eighty seven Earth days. A day on Jupiter is 9.8 Earth hours.

In reality there is no time, there is only eternity, timelessness. In the spirit world everything is happening simultaneously in the NOW. Eternity and timelessness are far beyond our ability as finite beings to comprehend. Don't drive yourself nuts trying to figure it all out. Time is another illusion of our five senses. (See Chapter 13, Meditation)

> The laws of science do not distinguish between the past and the future.
> ~Stephen Hawking

We Are One

We live in the universe and the universe is in us. Earth is a living being of which we are all part and is conscious through us. We come from the Earth; our minds are Earth's minds, our consciousness is Earth's consciousness. What we perceive as empty space, is consciousness without form. The universe is one seamless fabric of interconnected particles of energy uniting everyone and everything — including the most distant galaxies at the very edge of outer space. At our deepest level of being we are one with everyone and everything as expressions of Universal Intelligence.

Everyone around us is a projection of ourselves. We are all individual expressions of the same Divine Source. Our connections with each other are much deeper than we realize. These relationships transcend time and space, which are fragments of eternity. By living only in the one percent material world, we miss out on ninety-nine percent of what life has to offer.

There are many levels and layers to science and spirituality. Not until one layer is peeled away are we even aware of the next. Every time we remove one layer a deeper more meaningful one is revealed to us. We grow and evolve consciously and spiritually as each successive layer brings us closer to the heart of wisdom and truth. The next great frontier of exploration is not outer space; it is the exploration of inner space.

> Our challenge today is to move beyond the concepts and confines of religion into a direct encounter with spirituality.
> ~ *Carl Jung*

We use only ten percent of our brains' capacity. A Genius would use only about thirteen percent. Imagine how different the world would be today if mankind used the other ninety percent. All hostilities would end instantly. A deep sense of mission with a greater purpose would prevail. Everyone would join together to serve humanity and heal the planet. This is not an impossible dream of attainment. The only thing separating us from this becoming a reality is our desire to change and the courage to push boundaries. We must release the old ways of thinking and raise our level of consciousness. The chaos and suffering the world is experiencing today is the result of our limited awareness. This limited awareness is the result of self empowering truths that were suppressed by certain organizations and institutions to control people. These truths are essential to our spiritual growth and development.

Right now we have the opportunity to spiritually awaken and reclaim our divinity. Life becomes richer and more meaningful when we are awake. We have a clear understanding of who we are, where we are, and why we are here. We create harmony, healing, and balance for ourselves and those around us by making wiser choices and decisions. When we are awake we are able to actively participate in the shaping of our destiny and the destiny of the world.

All things are interconnected. What befalls the Earth befalls the sons and daughters of the Earth. We did not weave this web of life; we are merely a strand in it. Whatever we do to the web, we do to ourselves.
~Chief Seattle,
upon giving up his Pacific Northwest Tribal homeland to the White Man in 1854

Chapter 3
We are Creators

What we are today comes from
our thoughts of yesterday, and
our present thoughts build our
life of tomorrow: Our life is the
creation of our mind.
~Buddha

One of the most important self-empowering truths is the law of attraction. This powerful spiritual principle has been a closely guarded secret because of its awesome power. One percent of the Earth's population controls ninety five percent of the income, because they know how to use the law of attraction. Once we incorporate this way of thinking into our lives we move from the backseat into the driver's seat.

This is how the law of attraction operates. Our thoughts and feelings create our world. In other words, what we think, feel, and put our energy into, whether negative or positive, we draw to us like magnets. Our thoughts and feelings are energy vibrations constantly projected into the universe. We create change in our lives through the power of our imagination and emotions. Our thoughts and feelings are messages broadcast into the universe which responds by manifesting them. Our thoughts become things. It doesn't matter what our present circumstances may be or where we are in life right now. When we change our thoughts we change our reality.

Remember, we are One with the universe. Our bodies and minds are made of stardust. As conscious beings we are the universe knowing itself. The universe responds to our thoughts and feelings by creating what we program it to do.

The universe will create what we are thinking about whether we want it or not. Negative thoughts and emotions prevent us from creating the life of our dreams. Sometimes we think about things we don't want and draw them to us while pushing away the things we do want. We can use the law of attraction to push away the things we don't want and draw to us the things we do. The universe will mirror back to us what we project into it.

Our lives are like clay on a table. We shape our lives with our minds instead of our hands. We must learn to develop our powers of thought in order to live rich and meaningful lives.

We are the author, director, and actor of our life. Hence negative thoughts bring negative results. What we call bad luck is the direct result of negative thoughts and feelings. The first step to healing is doing away with limiting thoughts and behaviors of the ego. We gain clarity and insight when we replace the ego with our higher self. We connect with inner guidance and wisdom and visualize ourselves as we want to be. In a peaceful meditative state of consciousness, we give this mental image shape and form.

We are divine beings with unlimited potential made in the image and likeness of God. We possess the divine attributes of the Creator. We have infinite resources to co-create the lives we desire.

The key to the law of attraction is to visualize what we want with sincere desire and a deep sense of gratitude. The universe will create pathways for us to receive it. The mind shapes our universe. We are not potential creators because we are always creating. Now is the time to create the life we want by using the law of attraction. It's not just thinking about something. We need to envision results as we would like them with a deep sense of gratitude. Then watch them manifest as they are drawn into our lives.

> Whether you think you can or you can't either way you are right.
> ~ Henry Ford

Universe Gives Back Our Thoughts

We send thought impulses out into the universe and it transforms those thoughts into our reality. If we constantly think about being in debt the universe will respond to those thoughts by making sure we stay in debt. If you think about being a victim of bad luck the universe will create situations to sustain our bad luck mentality because like attracts like. Our life can be terrific or it can be turmoil. We are the ones responsible for creating the world we live in.

The situations in our lives at the present moment are the result of our thoughts from the past. In order to change our situation we must change the quality of thoughts we project. Circumstances and situations we want in life are either attracted to us or repelled from us depending on our mindset. It is our passion which makes all the difference and it begins with the choices we make. When we raise our level of awareness we make wiser choices and decisions.

First we must project love and respect to the world and treat others the way we want to be treated. What we give to others we get back in return. So when we project love and respect we receive love and respect. Once we start to see positive results from using this powerful law, we can apply it to all areas of our life.

The skeptic says, "I'll believe it when I see it."

The mystic says, "I'll see it when I believe it."

Every time we find ourselves thinking a negative thought, we need to stop immediately, delete it, and replace it with a positive thought. Positive thoughts are a hundred times more powerful than negative thoughts. We must cut off our reactive nature (the ego) and become proactive (the higher self). We can change every aspect of our life for the better by utilizing the law of attraction.

> Follow your bliss and the uni-
> verse will open doors for you
> where before there were only
> walls.
>   ~*Joseph Campbell*

Loving people live in a loving world. Angry people live in a hostile world. All of the negative energy being generated in the world is manifested in the state of the world today. By controlling the negative thoughts projected into the universe we can make our lives heaven or hell. Unfortunately ninety-nine percent of the world population is completely unaware of the law of attraction.

Everything in the universe is energy; we control that energy by controlling our thoughts. All power comes from within us and is therefore under our control. We are the creators of our destiny by the power of thought. We are the ones who create our reality. We must take responsibility for everything and every situation in our life, especially the most chaotic. We must stop the mind from generating old worn out thought patterns which created this turmoil.

We Must First Understand Our Thoughts

Once we understand the universe responds to our thoughts to create our world we can use this amazing power to draw to us the life we desire. This includes everything; our relationships, jobs, health, abundance, life enhancing opportunities and experiences if it is for our highest good. We are Divine Beings with unlimited potential to build our life according to our designs.

> The best way to predict the future is to create it.
> ~ *Peter F. Drucker*

The most powerful way to transform our lives is with gratitude. Without gratitude there will be no change. The master teachers from every religious tradition throughout time have all demonstrated the power of gratitude in their life.

We begin by making a list of everything for which we are grateful. The roofs over our heads, the beds we sleep in, the food we eat, and the air we breathe. With a deep sense of gratitude, we need to focus on every item one by one and feel the sense of inner peace, joy, and appreciation it brings us. By radiating inner feelings of gratitude and appreciation the universe will attract things from the outside to us which will support our gratitude and appreciation.

Gratitude for the abundance we have received will ensure the abundance will continue. In life we fail to realize we receive a great deal more than we give.

We are the ones in control once we understand the law of attraction.

Mankind can change the destiny of the world by utilizing the law of attraction collectively. Individually we are like fragile snowflakes. But enough snowflakes in one place can create a blizzard which could shut down a city. The world benefits when we are at our best because we contribute to the greater good of everyone collectively on this living, breathing spaceship we call planet Earth.

> Imagination is everything; it is the preview of life's coming attractions.
> ~*Albert Einstein*

Chapter 4
The New God

All the cosmos is a single substance of which we are part.
God is not an external manifes-
tation, but everything that is.
~ *Spinoza*

As a child I was taught God was an old man with a
long white beard sitting on a cloud far away in
heaven. He would watch us from above and happily reward us for being good, or angrily punish us if we
were bad.

After death we would meet the Almighty and be
judged according to our actions here on Earth. If we lived
a good life we would go to heaven forever. If we lived a
bad life, we would burn in hell forever. I was taught God
is all loving and merciful and yet at the same time cruel
and unforgiving.

Think about this...

If we make God happy by doing good things, and make God angry by doing bad things, this would mean that *we control God*. We can make God have a good day or we can make God have a bad day depending on our actions. To think that humans have the power to control God's emotions is absurd. Human beings cannot control God.

Consider this:

Imagine we were sitting around a campfire. We would be able to cook our food on the fire; use the light to see in the dark, and the heat to keep us warm. We receive all the benefits of the fire. But if we put our hands into the fire, we would get burned. Does this mean the fire is angry at us for touching it, and punished us? Of course it doesn't. It simply means that if we put our hands in the flames, we experience pain.

God is like a fire. When we live within the principles and the properties of the Creator, we enjoy all the benefits. When we go against those principles and properties, it's like sticking our hands into the flames. God does not punish us, *we punish ourselves*. The Creator is not an external man we are going to meet after death. The Creator is internal, both *Father and Mother*. We do not have to wait until we die to meet God. We can enjoy God's presence every moment of every day, because God is everything there is. Every step we take is on holy ground. Every breath we take is sacred. There is as much of God in a single blade of grass as there is in all the cathedrals on Earth.

We do not have to go anywhere to meet God. If there was a place where God could not be, that would mean

God is limited. What kind of God would be limited? That is absolutely ridiculous.

When we study all the world's major religious traditions we discover they are all sewn together with common threads of unconditional love, compassion, forgiveness, and that we are ONE. *We are all individual expressions of the same Divine Source.* Just as all the vibrant colors of a rainbow are contained in a single beam of white sunlight. We are one.

We are all branches on the same tree. When we judge other people, we judge ourselves. When we hurt other people, we hurt ourselves. When we help other people we help ourselves. The greatest commandment of all is "love thy neighbor as thyself."

This is what Master Teacher Jesus meant when he said, "Know the truth and the truth will set you free." When we know our true relationship with the Creator as the Divine beings we truly are, we will be free from all the fear, guilt, myths, and superstition that blind us. Jesus was talking about spiritual freedom, self-empowerment, and the fact that *we are all the sons and daughters of God.*

> The Spiritual Externalist waits reunification with God after death, while the Internalist feels part of the Oneness each and every day.
> *~Unknown*

We are spiritual beings created from the very essence of Divinity. God's spirit is all power and all wisdom moving within us and expressing as us at all times and in all circumstances. The Divine Presence is our constant companion, the ultimate resource of all wisdom and joy providing us with unlimited potential to live rich and meaningful lives.

There is No Final Judgment

Many people fear a final judgment with punishing tribunals at death. Hellfire, brimstone, and eternal damnation would put the fear of God into anyone. What kind of God would say to his children: "If you make an error in your one short lifetime, you will burn in hell for all eternity to pay for it"? Religious authorities have turned the Almighty, all powerful, all loving and merciful God into a cruel and loveless sociopath.

When we return home at death we go through a process where we get to see our life through everyone else's eyes. We see where we did well in life and where we could have done a whole lot better. We feel the joy and the pain our words and actions brought other people in a way we could never have known when we were here. It is not a final judgment with punishing tribunals as organized religion tells us, rather it is a *life review*.

Do you know who the most severe critic is during the review? We are. We don't regret so much the things we did when we were here, as the things we did not do.

We are expected to make mistakes in life in order to learn from them. We are given every opportunity to correct them for our spiritual growth and development through reincarnation.

God didn't create punishment and reward laws for us to follow. Religious authorities who wanted to control their congregations made the punishment and reward laws. God is not loveless and cruel. The time has come to stop living in the dark ages with these outdated codes and rules designed to control our ancestors. We must stop expecting the Creator to act like a human being filled with wants and desires.

Instead we must claim our Divine inheritance by moving beyond the walls of fear and guilt. We must not let outdated myths and superstitions keep us from connecting directly with the Creator. All the great master teachers tell us look within for this Divine connection. Happiness and security are our birthright as children of God.

It is foolish and immature to measure our relationship with God through material possessions. God does not reward us with material possessions and punish us by taking them away. Our progress on the spiritual path is not represented by events or material things. God's message is not meant to condemn, punish or destroy; but to educate, correct and heal.

There is only one Source, One Spirit. God and creation are One. If we want to look into the Creator's eyes; look into each other's eyes. The illusion of separation fades away on higher levels of consciousness. Everything in the universe is an extension of everything else.

Scientists and sages agree that the universe is made of a single seamless fabric in which we are all woven together. Anything with the appearance of separation of consciousness and matter is merely an illusion. God is the essence of all form, *including us*. Realizing this profound and wonderful truth opens the doors to the mysteries of creation.

When we raise our consciousness and open our hearts as the master teachers Jesus, Buddha, Krishna, and Moses have shown us through their example; we become conduits for the power of the Divine Source. Just as electricity lights a lamp, Divine power lights our soul. Illuminated, we reflect this magnificent, powerful, and loving Divine Light into the world through kind words, actions, compassion, charity, and forgiveness. This is how we light up the world. This is the path to awakening.

Ice Cubes and Ocean Are Not Separate

Imagine that the spirit world is the ocean. We take some water from the ocean and freeze it into ice cubes. Then we take those ice cubes and put them back in the ocean. Are not the ice cubes also the ocean? Of course they are. But for a short time they are under the illusion of being separate and apart from the ocean. After a while the ice cubes melt and return to the ocean.

We are like those ice cubes here on earth. We are under the illusion of being separate from the spirit world, our departed family and friends and the infinite love and light of the Creator, when in fact we are right in the middle of it! We are not ice cubes we are the ocean. The key is to wake up to the fact we are ocean while we are still here, to realize we are home right now.

It is an illusion we are separate and apart from the spirit world. If there were spirit glasses we could wear and see everyone around us, all our fears would instantly melt away. But we don't have spirit glasses. We have to *trust* we have their love and support in spite of the fact we can't see them or hear them clearly. We also need to trust the Divine Presence of God is with us always.

If we die before *we wake* up, it's too late. We get to see all the powers, abilities, and tools we could have used in life that no one ever told us we had. We would say, "I could've had a totally different experience had I known I had these powers and abilities!" We'd see all the different roads we could have taken on our journey through life. It is in our best interest to wake up while we are here, learn our lessons now so we don't have to return, and take this class again. We are here at the Earth School to learn how to get out of here. How many lifetimes it will take is up to us. The first thing we must do is wake up.

I'll give you another example: Imagine there is a nuclear reactor that supplied all the electricity for the United States. All of the energy generated at the reactor was distributed to every household from coast to coast. All electrical appliances in our house rely on the energy coming from this one single source.

Does this mean we can take our alarm clock to the nuclear reactor and plug it in directly? Of course not, the tiny alarm clock would literally vaporize. The energy is much too powerful at the source.

All of the energy coming from the nuclear reactor is broken down to a manageable frequency through a series of resistors before it is delivered to our homes. We cannot take our appliances directly to the nuclear reactor and plug them in.

The Creator is like a nuclear reactor. There are a series of spiritual resistors (places, levels, planes, dimensions) breaking down the awesome power of God into a manageable frequency we use in the physical world.

This is what Jesus was referring to during the Last Supper when he said "In my Father's house there are many mansions." Spirits reside within a multitude of places (levels, planes, dimensions) within the Kingdom of Heaven.

Cracks let Light Drip Away

The Light of God comes from God the same way sunlight comes from the Sun. Sunlight is not the Sun. Sunlight comes from the Sun. The Light of God is not God, it comes from God. God is the source of everything, everywhere, without exception.

God's Light is shining on us at all times. It always has been and always will be. We never have to ask God to shine Light on us. All we need to do is be open to receive it and absorb it into our body, mind and soul.

This is an example:

Pour hot water into a mug. The mug takes on the properties of the water and gets hot. The mug radiates with heat. The larger the mug the more water it would hold. If the mug was cracked the water would leak out. The more cracks it had, the faster water would drain out.

Our souls are vessels like that mug. When we fill ourselves with God's Light we absorb it into every ounce of our being. We take on the properties of this Divine Light. We radiate and reflect God's Light into the world. The more open we are to receive Divine Light, the more our soul will hold.

Anger, resentment, fear, and negativity are cracks in our soul. The more negative energy we have the more cracks there are. We must mend those cracks in order to hold and absorb the properties of the Creator. We do this through acts of kindness, charity, compassion, and forgiveness. We become clear reflectors of God's Love and Light into the world. We are the light of the world. We are God learning to be God.

It's imperative to give heartfelt thanks for our blessings and share them with others. We must allow our true spiritual nature to shine through. We must not define ourselves by who we are, but by *what we are*, our spiritual essence. We must share our knowledge, gifts, and talents with others. The more we give, the more we receive. No supply is ever depleted when it is given freely from the heart.

Much is gained when we share generously with one another. Acts of kindness and charity influence other people in a positive way. This makes life richer and more meaningful. Higher levels of consciousness are revealed on the path of spiritual discovery.

Religious Rehab

Today there are a growing number of rehabilitation centers for alcoholics and drug addicts. But there should also be rehabilitation centers for organized religion.

- ❖ First you have a Spiritual intervention.
- ❖ Then you go through detox and purge your mind of all the erroneous doctrines and dogma.

❖ After the detox you wake up clear and free from all the fear, guilt and false beliefs.
❖ Next you recover all your God-given powers and abilities.
❖ Then you reclaim your true spiritual identity as a Divine Being with unlimited potential able to live a rich and meaningful life.

My name is Alan and I am a recovering Catholic.

The Dark Side is Ignorance

There is a dark side that needs to be respected, but not feared. The dark side is ignorance and absence of light. Divine Light is infinitely more powerful than the dark side. All the darkness of the world cannot put out the light of a single candle. We are at the Earth School to use our freewill to choose between good and evil, the light and the dark for spiritual growth and development. We would not have the opportunity to exercise our freewill if there was only Light.

The dark side gives us the opportunity overcome challenges of these apparent opposites. We use our spiritual power to rise above temptation and connect with the light within. How else can we discover the level of our courage and strength without darkness?

> Evil (ignorance) is like a shadow. It has no real substance of its own; it is simply a

lack of light. You cannot cause
a shadow to disappear by trying
to fight it, stamp on it, by rail-
ing against it, or any other form
of emotional or physical resis-
tance. In order to cause a
shadow to disappear, you must
shine light on it.
~ *Shakti Gawain*

The World of Opposites

On earth we perceive life as a world of opposites and
dualities — light and dark, good and evil, male and female, tall and short, thick and thin, hot and cold. But each
one depends on the other for its very existence. How
could we know happiness if we did not know sorrow? On
earth we experience everything by contrast. These dualities do not exist in the spirit world where there is only
Light. We cannot experience fear, pain, sorrow, anger,
jealousy, despair, greed or anything negative at home in
the Light.

The truth is there are no real dualities. How can you
have an inside without an outside? Up without down?
Tall without short? How can we have a giver without a
receiver? One would be meaningless without the other.
All of these apparent dualities are actually part of the
same whole.

Draw a circle on a piece of paper. Now make one half
of the circle. You can't make one half, because the mo-

ment you draw a line down the center of the circle you create two halves. You can't have one half of something without the other half.

Light and dark are not separate entities. Darkness is a place where it is very hard to see light and the light is a place where it is very hard to see darkness. Good is a place where it is hard to see evil, and evil is a place where it's hard to see goodness. Hot is a place of very little cold and vice versa. All opposites are part of the same whole. Each extreme expression is a necessary part of the whole. Duality is merely another illusion on Earth because we cannot see the big picture.

We are not separate from God. There is nothing between us and the Creator. We cannot separate ourselves from the Divine Source. We are One. Every star, every person, every blade of grass is a perfect expression of the Creator in form.

The following prayer says it most succinctly:

Lords Prayer, from the original Aramaic
Translation by Neil Douglas-Klotz in Prayers of the Cosmos

O Birther! Father- Mother of the Cosmos
Focus your light within us - make it useful.
Create your reign of unity now-
through our fiery hearts and willing hands
Help us love beyond our ideals
and sprout acts of compassion for all creatures.
Animate the earth within us: we then
feel the Wisdom underneath supporting all.
Untangle the knots within

so that we can mend our hearts' simple ties to each other.
Don't let surface things delude us,
But free us from what holds us back from our true purpose.
Out of you, the astonishing fire,
Returning light and sound to the cosmos.
Amen.

Chapter 5

Trust

We cannot discover new oceans
until we have the courage to
loose sight of the shore.
~ *Andre Gide*

Faith and belief are quite different from trust. Certain beliefs can be changed or proven wrong. To believe in God is to aspire to an unseen force that we hope is out there watching over us. We have faith that God will answer our prayers. Trust however is much stronger than faith or belief.

Trust is a giant step beyond faith and belief; it is a deep realization of God. With trust there is no conscious separation from God. Trust cannot be shaken by doubt and fear. Trust is working with an unseen force we *know* is always with us and we *know* will answer our prayers. We *trust* the all-knowing and all-powerful spirit of the Creator is working with us and through us. After all, we are manifestations of God's thoughts.

"In God We Trust" is found on the back of our one dollar bill. It does not mean in God we trust Savings and Loan. Our founding fathers did not say, "We believe God is with us," or "We have faith that God is watching over us." They simply chose in "God We Trust."

I never really fully appreciated the true meaning of trust until I began walking the spiritual path. I developed a deeper appreciation and respect for our founding fathers. They were saying. "We *know* God is with us." In its infancy America knew the deeper meaning of trust. That is why our founding fathers chose trust over belief and faith. Without trust we still would be living under the British flag. Winning our independence from England required an immense amount of trust in God.

> All that I have seen teaches me
> to trust the Creator I have not
> seen.
> *~Ralph Waldo Emerson*

Trust is the Magic Ingredient

(Metaphorically speaking) Trust is walking up to the edge of a cliff and stepping off knowing that one of two things will happen: a bridge will form beneath our feet, or we will learn to fly. Trust is not walking to the cliff and looking up to the heavens and asking God to show us the bridge. Trust is stepping off the cliff *knowing* a bridge will appear. Once we step off a cliff in trust and learn how to fly, it will be easier and faster when we come to the next cliff because we learned the true meaning of trust. *Trust is the magic ingredient.* Unfortunately most people are afraid to trust. Only when we have the courage to move out of our comfort zones are we able to grow. Trust is the magic ingredient that makes all the difference. Put a little magic in life today and see what happens.

> Avoiding danger is no safer in the long run than outright exposure. Life is either a daring adventure or it is nothing.
> *~Helen Keller*

One of my favorite stories from the Old Testament is Moses releasing the chosen people from bondage in Egypt. I was told as a child that Moses asked God to save the Israelites from the Egyptians and God parted the Red Sea so everyone could escape. But later I learned that's not what really happened.

Moses and the Israelites were standing on the shore of the Red Sea. The Egyptians were hot on their tails and everyone was near panic. Moses knew a Sacred Code that would overcome the laws of Mother Nature and part the Red Sea. He spread his arms over the sea and used the code to part the water. You know what happened? Absolutely nothing happened. Moses knew he used the sacred code exactly right and he dared not use it again. It was not until people started walking into the water…not up to their knees, not up to their chests, not until the water was up to the tips of their noses that the final element of the sacred code was in place. Do you know what the final element was? It was trust. When trust was established, the water parted. Through trust in God their lives were saved and they were able to enter into the Promised Land as well as their next stage of spiritual awareness.

With trust in the Creator we are able to participate in shaping our destiny. Trust is the sacred element needed to move beyond the boundaries and borders of fear. It gives us courage and strength to do what we love; life is too short to do anything else. We access our true potential when we take the first step forward and it's going to require trust. Trust is the magic that makes all the difference in life. That's way we are here at school. It's easy to connect the dots from the past by looking backward in life. We have to trust the dots will connect in our future. We must thank God for our blessings and trust God for our needs.

With trust we *know* we have our invisible spiritual support team guiding and protecting us at all times. We have Spirit Guides and Guardian Angels who will inspire us to move in certain directions or not move in other directions. Trusting our intuition, our gut feelings will help us make better choices and decisions. How many times have you gone against those feelings only to regret it later? I have many times.

With this deeper wisdom we reach higher levels of awareness and realize our true relationship with God. The path to awakening is paved with trust. God works through us co-creating our lives when we are open and aware. Through trust we know we are being guided to our highest destiny.

We must not let other people's limited perceptions define us. Our time on Earth is short. Don't waste it by living someone else's dream. We must find what we love and pursue it with passion, not settling until we achieve our dreams. Each of us must ask. "If today was the last day of my life what would I do over?" Let that be a guide and follow our dream. It is essential to trust the inner guidance and wisdom we receive with all our heart. We are bigger and more powerful than we think.

> We all know what we are; we
> don't know what we can be.
> ~William Shakespeare

Chapter 6
Ego and Higher Self

He that falls in love with himself will have no rivals.
~*Benjamin Franklin*

We come to earth with two sources of input on our journey through life. Zen Buddhists call them the *small mind* and *Big Mind*. Small mind is the *ego* and Big Mind is the *higher self*. The ego is self-centered, controlling, fearful, superficial, compulsive, and reactive. It is our *lower self*. The Higher Self is kind, compassionate, forgiving, proactive, and is our direct connection to the Divine Source. The Higher Self is our truest essence and our most perfect form.

Unfortunately, our society encourages us to have strong egos to function competitively and aggressively. We judge success by the size of salaries and houses rather than by the quality of service and relationship to humanity. We get lost in the illusions of the physical world, paying homage to material possessions. Jealousy of others' lifestyles, appearances, and possessions supports selfish egos in separating us from our true spiritual essence. The contrast between these levels of awareness could mean the difference between heaven and hell.

The ego places itself at the center of the universe around which everything revolves. When we identify with the ego we experience separation and limitation. We live in a world of form, illusion, fear, and pain. The ego has many identities: ethnic, financial, social, sexual, racial, job, physical, religious and more.

What separates us from the higher self is our level of awareness. The higher self is our direct connection to the Creator and identifies with unity consciousness. By raising our consciousness we release the ego's grip gaining greater insight into our life and the roles we play. The higher self serves as a guide to help us make wiser choices and decisions. It knows us far better than we know ourselves. Humanity's higher selves are all interconnected forming a field of collective consciousness. It is a matrix/shield of Divine Light and Order surrounding and protecting the planet.

Our life on earth is the classroom for us to grow in wisdom as we bring our body and soul into divine union. Our greatest challenge is bringing this higher awareness to our conscious mind.

We can make our lives miserable or make it meaningful; either takes the same amount of work. The choice is ours. The worst enemy we have to deal with in life is the one we see in the mirror. There is always a tug-of-war between small mind and Big Mind... *between me and we.*

The ego is the image of self-importance we show the world. The ego is motivated by fear and believes it is separate. The ego sees in itself what others cannot see. The ego (our lower self) has limited access to information because it relies only on the five senses and its observations in the material world. It desperately searches for security, self-enhancement, and survival.

The small mind seeks things it does not possess, and is then enslaved by the very things it acquires. The question is, do we have possessions or do the possessions have us? The ego is in control when we struggle to do more and have more. The ego is as real as we let it be and responds reactively to anything that threatens its self-image. It stays alive in its victim consciousness by being attached to the past and afraid of change. When we engage the ego it becomes stronger. It seeks external power and has an insatiable appetite. The more we feed the ego the hungrier it gets. But that hunger can never be satisfied. There is one good thing about an egotist: they never go around talking about anyone else.

After experiencing enough chaos and pain, we let go of the illusion of separation to embrace unity and wholeness. We shift away from the self-centered ego. We find our way back home to the power, love, and wisdom of the soul. This is the path of the higher self.

Whenever the ego rears its ugly head in whatever forms it takes (fear, insecurity, judgment, resentment, envy, calculating, compulsive, reactive etc.) recognize it for what it is and then let it go. This allows the higher self to take over.

I press a delete button in my mind when ego-based

thoughts suddenly appear. The small mind is a major obstacle on the spiritual path because of its self-centered,
superficial, unenlightened perception. Releasing the
ego's grip is the first step on the spiritual path and it will
fight for survival every inch of the way.

> There is no room for God in
> him who is full of himself.
> ~*Hasidic saying*

The higher self is our true spiritual identity and the
very essence of our being. It is motivated by love, has
enlightened perception and unity consciousness. The
higher self appreciates beauty, has courage to take risks,
the capacity to sacrifice, and a strong desire to be of service to others. It wants to share freely without attach-
ments. It doesn't chase after money or worry about
failure.

The ego is in love with external power, a weakness
disguised as strength. The higher self is the power of love
within, and it is always available. We need to develop
our ability to listen to our higher self. We do this by examining our motives. We must ask ourselves, "Are we
motivated by love or are we motivated by fear?" We get
a better picture of ourselves when we observe what ag-
gravates us about other people.

Human beings are like a one-car garage. There is room
for either our ego or higher self; not both. If we choose the
ego we have chosen to live in the limiting, superficial illusions of the material world. We will have more struggles
with ourselves than any other person in life.

- We can purchase our dream house, but not a happy home.
- We can purchase a comfortable bed, but not a sound sleep.
- We can purchase meaningless sex, but not unconditional love.
- We can purchase an extensive library, but not a drop of wisdom.
- We can purchase powerful positions, but not an ounce of respect.
- We can purchase an expensive watch, but not one second of time.

The ego relates to the thin outer shell, the veneer, the sparkle and shine. There is no substance to support the superficial ego. It is a castle made of sand. The higher self on the other hand, constantly challenges us to open to the big picture and deeper meaning. If you want to feel wealthy, count all the things you have in life that money can't buy.

Humanity is evolving from survival of the fittest to survival of the wisest. Internal power of the soul is far superior to an external power of the body. With greater awareness humanity will take its next evolutionary step forward recognizing the body and soul as one being. All the ancient wisdom traditions tell us we must transcend our attachment to the ego to reach Enlightenment. The death of the ego opens our minds to the entire universe and beyond. We don't have to change what we see, only how we see it. The beginning of wisdom is to desire it.

We must ask ourselves, "Where am I on the path?"

Collectively we can make this world a better place by following the inner guidance of the higher self. When we remove the ego, we move beyond our struggle for personal identity. When we are all wrapped up in our self, we make a very small package.

We can't go back in time and make a brand new start, but we can start from this point and make a brand new ending. The higher self is our eternal spiritual identity and our direct connection with the Divine Source. When we dedicate our lives to something greater than ourselves we find meaning and self-worth. The meaning of life is to give life meaning. We bring meaning, purpose and joy to our lives by engaging in acts of kindness, compassion, and service to others. And remember it's the journey that brings us happiness not the destination.

EGO = Edge God Out
EGO = Everybody's Got One

Chapter 7
Reincarnation

It is not more surprising to be
born twice than once; everything in nature is resurrection.
~ *Voltaire*

Have you ever wondered why life is so unfair?

Why are some people born into a life of struggle and others of privilege?

Why God makes one person a genius and another with Down syndrome?

Why are some born strong and others weak?

What happened? Did God run out of all the healthy, wealthy bodies?

Consider this: When our children were learning how to walk and they fell, did we pick them up and help them until they got strong and learned to walk? Of course. Why? Because we love our children. We didn't say to the child after they fell down the first time, "Well, there you go; that was your one chance to walk and you blew it! Now you have to sit there the rest of your life!" That's absurd. We picked up the child and gave them another chance, and another and another. Eventually the child became strong enough to stand up and walk on their own.

We are all God's children and when we fall down during a lifetime, we are given another chance to get it right. And another and another and another, because *God loves us*. It may take many lifetimes to learn a lesson, but once we learn it, we learn it for eternity. We won't need to come back and take that class again.

The Eyes are the Windows to the Soul

What kind of God would let young children die of cancer? What did they do to deserve this? These innocent young children are actually highly evolved souls who chose that incarnation knowing full well they were going to be here for a short time and leave in that way. *They came here to teach*, not to learn. They are called "Teacher Souls." These advanced souls teach us about unconditional love, compassion, courage and strength. We're taught how precious life is and that tomorrow is promised to no one. All we need to do is look into their eyes and we can see they are *old souls*, because *the eyes are the windows to the soul*.

Have you ever noticed people with Down syndrome are some of the happiest people on the face of the earth? They too are evolved souls who came here to teach.

Geniuses are not necessarily evolved souls; they are

just smart people. Just because someone has a high IQ doesn't mean they are more spiritually evolved than someone with Down syndrome.

When we observe life from a higher level of awareness, we have a clearer view of the big picture. We have a deeper understanding of what is actually unfolding and why bad things happen to good people.

> Souls are poured from one into another of different kinds of bodies of the world.
> ~*Jesus the Christ in Gnostic Gospels: Pistis Sophia*

It's impossible for us to learn all of the lessons about love and forgiveness in just one lifetime, in one dynamic. We come back over and over again as male, female, tall, short, weak, strong, healthy, sick, rich, poor, in all cultural backgrounds and religious traditions. Being in many different bodies, cultures, and dynamics expands the nature of our Soul. The primary function of reincarnation is to allow our souls to experience all sides of all situations in every conceivable role.

Our life experiences are rich in diversity by design enabling us to have a well-rounded education. The multitude of lives we live broadens our Soul's experience. We hone our skills and learn a variety of lessons over many lifetimes. As our souls mature we make better choices and decisions enabling us to get the most out of every life we live. Our higher self knows what we need. Not to be happy, but to grow and evolve spiritually. The soul occupies many different bodies on its journey through eternity.

Everything in life follows the law of cycles. Seasons change in cycles, the sun rises and sets in cycles, plants flower and bloom in cycles, people are born and die in cycles. The universal law of cycles includes reincarnation. Reincarnation gives us the ability to become all that we are capable of becoming. We do not remain in one place where there is no opportunity for growth. We are divine beings and reincarnation enables us to realize our full potential. At that point there is no need to reincarnate as physical forms and we can move on to the upper realms in the spirit world. Reincarnation offers us the opportunity to correct mistakes made in the past. This is done through the law of karma. Karma is explained in the next chapter.

We All Experience Déjà vu

Sometimes fragments of our past life memories are jarred to the surface by familiar surroundings or people and we experience déjà vu. We have a compelling feeling of already having experienced or seen something which in actuality is being experienced for the first time in our lives. Many people have experienced déjà vu when visiting a new city or country. They have an uncanny knowledge of a new place, knowing what was just around the corner on a road in a place they have never visited before. These are fragments of past life memories of a landscape or town. We don't make the connections because we are only getting bits and pieces of these memories, but we know we have been there before. Déjà vu can be described as "remembering pieces of the past."

Sometimes, we have a strong connection to certain geographical locations and historical events. Visiting the pyramids in Egypt or the Acropolis in Greece can be like a homecoming. Perhaps there is a strong connection to an historical event like the Civil War or the sinking of the Titanic. Many Americans have past life connections with Native American tribes through reincarnation. Even Jesus spoke about reincarnation in the Bible.

> But I tell you, Elijah has al-
> ready come, and they did not
> recognize him, but have done to
> him everything they wished. In
> the same way the Son of Man is
> going to suffer at their hands.'
> Then the disciples understood
> that he was talking to them
> about John the Baptist.
> ~*Jesus the Christ,*
> *(Matthew 17:12, 13)*

The early Christian Church teachings included reincarnation. During the Second Ecumenical Council of Constantinople in 553 A.D. church leaders removed all references to reincarnation. They replaced it with the myth of one life to live using heaven and hell as rewards and punishments to control the flock. Church leaders in the fourth century said reincarnation gave mankind too much time to gain salvation so it was edited and declared heresy. (Move over Galileo, make room for some more heresy)

The whole idea of the one life fable was to create a sense of urgency sending a message that the faithful would go to heaven forever and everyone else would suffer torments in hell for eternity.

Think about this: Hell is never mentioned once in the Old Testament; it suddenly appears out of nowhere in the New Testament. During the time of Jesus, original sin was called the "Original Blessing of Life." This was turned into a sin in the New Testament. All of a sudden according to religious authorities we are born sinners and will burn in hell forever if we don't watch out. Fear and guilt are powerful tools used to control people.

Man, Not God Made Religion

Any organization, institution, group or person withholding information from the congregation has an agenda to stay in power. People in power will suppress self-empowering information to prevent people under their control from leaving. Self-empowered people know their true relationship with the Creator and that is bad for business. Remember this: man, not God, made religion.

> The finger that points at the
> moon is not the moon.
> ~ *Zen saying*

To this day wars are fought over religious beliefs; each

side declares they are fighting for "God and Country." Nazi soldiers wore belt buckles with "GOT MITT UNS" (God with us) over a swastika. What a joke! God has nothing to do with war. Religious zealots and extremists that claim they are fighting for God do not even know what God is. "Holy War" is an oxymoron. There is nothing holy about mass murder. That is why one of the Ten Commandments is "thou shall not kill."

> We have guided missiles and misguided men.
> ~Martin Luther King Jr.

In the endless world, our true home, there is only love, compassion, forgiveness, and joy beyond measure. All negative energy is only found on this side of the veil. Heaven is closeness to God in consciousness. Hell is distance from God in consciousness. Heaven and hell are not places of rewards and punishment. They are states of mind.

There are a host of suppressed truths. Reincarnation is one of them. Most of the bloodshed throughout history could have been avoided if people had a clear understanding about reincarnation and the law of Karma. The more we understand about our true connections to each other, the more loving and compassionate we become.

There are highly evolved souls who reincarnate to walk among us. They are the Mystics, Masters, Saints and Sages who return to earth as teachers and healers. Buddhist, Christian, Hindu, Hebrew, or whatever religious tradition, whether speaking of God or Christ, Emptiness or Vastness, Rama or Allah, Universal Consciousness or the Divine One, these great beings show us the way to inner peace, self-realization and enlightenment. They guide us along the path to awakening. We have the power to end the cycle of reincarnation by following their example of expressing unconditional love, compassion, forgiveness and to be of service to other people. How long it will take is entirely up to us by the quality of our thoughts, words, and actions.

> All pure and holy spirits live on in heavenly places, and in course of time they are again sent down to inhabit righteous bodies
> ~*Jewish historian Josephus who lived around the time of Jesus*

We are here to learn how to get out of here. It is in our best interest to take responsibility for the conflicts and challenges we face in life. To learn our lessons now so we don't have to come back and repeat them in our next life. What we do in this life has a direct effect on our next life.

Think about this: Imagine we come to Earth as bright shining light bulbs. It is our job to leave here brighter than when we came. Say we came to earth as a twenty-five watt light bulb; it is our job to leave here at thirty or more watts. Whatever we leave at in this life, we come back at in our next life. This means if we come in as a twenty-five watt light, and leave as a thousand watt light we come back as a thousand watt in our next life. The brighter the light is, the higher the energy frequency. Spirits with high vibrations are evolved souls. They possess a deep understanding of truth and higher consciousness. The higher our vibration frequency is at birth, the sooner we start on the spiritual path.

Jesus, Buddha, Krishna, and Moses are perfect examples of evolved souls who came to inspire us, teach us, and show us the way to awaken our divine nature. These great spiritual teachers have achieved unlimited, unconditional love, universal compassion, profound peace, timeless wisdom, and truth. They light our way as we journey down the path to awakening.

> Thousands of candles can be lighted from a single candle, and the life of the candle will not be shortened. Happiness never decreases by being shared.
> ~Buddha

Sexuality Choices Made before We Are Born

We are spiritual beings occupying a human body. Spirits are androgynous. They vibrate with both masculine and feminine energy. Sex in the physical world is necessary for procreation. When spirits incarnate into human form, they tune in to one of those sexual polarities and enter the world as either a male or a female.

Sometimes a soul is born into a female body with a

masculine energy, and sometimes a soul is born into a male body with feminine energy. In fact, both male and female energies are contained in all of us and we are drawn to one polarity or the other, sometimes both. This is the underlying cause of homosexuality and bisexuality. These choices are made *before we are born* for the unique lessons those dynamics will provide the soul.

We have been here many times, and there are many reasons why we would volunteer to come back as a homosexual. Love is a diamond with many facets and homosexuality is one of them. Love is love. There are other reasons to return to Earth as a homosexual, including karma. Perhaps in a past life we persecuted homosexuals and we choose to learn about love from that perspective. There are myriad reasons why a soul and body match would be arranged this way. There are no accidents and no coincidences. Nothing is left to chance. In the physical world, we can't see the big picture.

Everything in our life charts is programmed to encourage us to wake up spiritually. We learn the deeper meaning behind the painful events. When we see bad things happen to good people it provides us with the opportunity to learn about kindness, compassion, patience, charity, sacrifice and forgiveness. How can we learn these priceless lessons if everything were perfect?

Consider the death of a child. Children are not supposed to die first. It's imperative for the bereaved parents to make every effort to find out where their child is. We are told they are either far away in heaven floating on a cloud, or burning in hell forever if the child committed suicide. The spirits of these young children are *right here with us* in a higher frequency of energy, in another dimension we call heaven. When the parents learn how the spirit world *really works* they are able to receive messages from their loved ones on the other side. Spirit communication and suicide are explained in later chapters.

On a higher level we benefit from overcoming trials, tribulations, and tragedies. When we return home we have something to show for the pain we endure. We are not here to suffer. There is a *divine order* behind everything we see as senseless suffering here on earth.

Life's Journey

It is not
for me to say
If I will
travel, again, this way
Whether I do or don't
is of no import
What matters is *how*
this life I court.
~*Beverly Miller*

Chapter 8
Karma

To conquer oneself is greater
than to conquer thousands in
battle.

~Buddha

When the early church leaders edited out all references to reincarnation, they also removed the law of karma. Everything we think, do, and say, has a consequence; for every cause there is an effect. Karma is the law of cause and effect that covers the actions of all life. What we do or cause in life carries with it the responsibility of its effect.

We label karma good or bad depending on whether it brings us pleasure or pain, but it is not a system of punishment and reward. We are responsible for the positive or negative effects our actions have on other people and how we respond to them. We must plant good seeds because the results of our actions return to us. One simple act of kindness can set off a chain reaction of kindness and generosity many times over. It also works the other way. How we treat others is our karma; how they react to us is their karma.

Karma is complex because it operates over many lifetimes. The cause and effects lay dormant until conditions are suitable to make corrections. With the law of karma we are born under circumstances which will create the best path to correct past errors. It is helpful for us to look at karma as an opportunity to learn spiritual lessons through trial and error rather than a system of reward and punishment. Even painful karma has its value in the development of the soul; it is a matter of interpretation. What might be initially interpreted as bad karma could actually be a blessing in disguise. My life is a perfect example. I was born with muscular dystrophy and I had a hard time keeping up with the other children my age. Playing sports was out of the question. No one wanted me on their team. I thought was being punished by God. I started asking spiritual questions at an early age. Why me? What did I do to deserve this? I wasn't able to get involved with physical activities. This provided me more time to read, meditate and search for answers. Over time my physical weakness was transformed into spiritual strength. I moved out a victim consciousness into higher levels of awareness. What I thought was bad karma initially, was actually a blessing in disguise. Having muscular dystrophy is a major challenge in my life, but I wouldn't trade it for all the spiritual strength it brought me. I know when I die I'll leave the muscular dystrophy behind and take what I've learned back home with me.

The universe is like a mirror that reflects the image we project including positive and negative energy. Our thoughts, feelings, and actions have roots in our past. A loving person lives in a loving world. An angry person lives in an angry world. Everyone we meet in life is our mirror. We constantly draw people into our lives that we need to learn from, educate, or both. We create our own reality.

The purpose of karma is to behave properly, or suffer the consequences. It's like sticking our hands into a fire; we punish ourselves. The effects of our actions create past, present, and future experiences. Everything we experience is determined by our soul, which reincarnates in order to end the wheel of karma.

Our soul's energy comes into the physical realm to work through its "Karmic" lessons, which are determined by our past thoughts and actions. Our thoughts and actions in this life have a direct effect on our future lives. Nothing is determined by chance; we must take personal responsibility for karmic fate.

Karma is the ultimate justice of the universe. There is no such thing as the "perfect crime." No one escapes karma. We all go home to the spirit world eventually. We all go through life reviews and will create new life charts with our Spirit Guides which will include the opportunities to pay back karmic debts. The master may volunteer to be the servant in a future lifetime to balance his or her karma. Karma returns to us in full and in-kind.

There are different types of karma:

- *Individual karma* involves our personal words and actions.

- *Family karma* includes the people we grow up with. We choose our parents and siblings for specific reasons. Nothing is left to chance.
- *Group karma* involves various organizations we belong to: ethnic, religious, racial, etc. We are connected to these groups by design.
- *National karma* includes all the people living in the country.
- *Human karma* involves the human race as a whole. We are part of a global family. The actions of individuals have an effect on the human race collectively.

We can condition our karma into a pattern of helping and healing others. Kindness and compassion gives our life meaning and serves our souls' purpose. Right now we have the opportunity to do away with all egotistical and self-destructive behavior. By recognizing negative patterns in our karmic journey we can alter our responses and make changes where necessary. With a positive change in attitude we program our Karma toward a much brighter future.

Recoding Karma

Every act and action in life creates karma. All karma must be balanced out in this or future lifetimes. We can "recode" negative karma we have created in this life by mentally revisiting past events that require forgiveness with a sincere feeling of sorrow for our harsh words and actions at our current level of spiritual awareness. Asking for forgiveness for our past words and actions connected to each event, we recode the karma which is attached to it. This is not to say the karma will be removed; it will be recoded. The karma attached to it will be lightened. Even if we are unable to speak to the person we can send those loving thoughts telepathically. Opportunities to forgive do not end at death.

As humans we only see bits and pieces of a much bigger picture. It's a waste of time trying to figure out all the mysteries of life and why bad things happen to good people. These fragmented events only appear as accidents or coincidences from our limited perspective. There is Divine Order behind everything we see as senseless suffering. We must surrender control over certain situations and realize we are magnificent divine beings either way. Love and respect are the greatest gifts we can offer one another.

> It is only when we realize that
> life is taking us nowhere that it
> begins to have meaning...
> ~ *P.D. Ospensky*

Chapter 9
Forgiveness

Forgiveness is the fragrance
that the violet sheds on the heel
that has crushed it.
~ *Mark Twain*

When we die and return home to the spirit world, we cannot bring anything with us, not even our bodies. We can only take what is inside. It is our mission to bring home as much love as possible and through forgiveness cut the ties to all the negative baggage we accumulate here. If we do not forgive, we drag that negative baggage home with us and we have to deal with it in a future life.

There is no escape. If we want to end destructive relationships and the karma attached to them, forgiveness is essential. There is a correct conclusion for every difficult situation we encounter. It is never too late to give or receive forgiveness; these opportunities do not end with death.

> An eye for an eye makes the
> whole world blind.
> ~ *Mahatma Gandhi*

People who antagonize us play very important roles in our life. They are essential for our spiritual development by teaching us to have courage, strength, wisdom, and patience. They challenge us to bring forgiveness into our lives and into the world. Without these challengers we would not be able to learn these priceless lessons.

Some of the greatest teachers in life are our enemies. They bring us face to face with fundamental choices between right and wrong. These people are often reflections of us and our deepest fears. Sometimes it's easy to forgive and other times it takes years. In the end it's all a matter of perspective. If we learn from these people, they are our teachers; if we don't learn they can stall our spiritual growth and development. Practicing practical applications of forgiveness guides us to the peace of mind we all seek.

Anger and resentment make us smaller. Forgiveness enables us to grow. The weight of confusion and concern are lifted and we experience serenity of the soul through forgiveness. When we plan to get even with someone, we are only letting that person continue to harm us.

Being kind is more important than being right. Without forgiveness our lives are governed by an endless cycle of anger and resentment. We cannot have lasting peace of mind without forgiveness. When we make forgiveness our primary goal, peace of mind will naturally follow. We forgive others when we let go of what they have done to us and focus on what we learned from the experience. This hard-won wisdom is the diamond in the heart of the lesson. We discover true inner peace when we base our lives on forgiving others and ourselves.

Through forgiveness we reclaim all the energy spent holding grudges and nursing old wounds. This energy is put to better use providing inner strength essential to free ourselves of negative thoughts and behaviors. Forgiveness has enormous healing power. It is linked to our physical, mental, and emotional well-being. We compromise our health by hanging onto past hurts. Blaming others for whatever is wrong in our life builds a foundation of bitterness and depression. Sometimes the only remedy for our suffering is forgiveness. Do it for yourself if not for the other person. People are healed when they *give the gift of forgiveness.*

We do not have to speak to or see that person in order to free ourselves. The path to reconciliation is thought and intention rather than a particular action. Forgiveness mends separation and promotes unity offering everyone involved a chance to do better. *Forgiveness is the key to universal happiness.*

> As long as you don't forgive, who and whatever it is will occupy rent-free space in your mind.
> ~Isabelle Holland

Every now and then we make mistakes and get knocked down in life. It is essential to get back up and focus on what we learned from those experiences. Resentment, fear, and guilt release their tight grip when we forgive ourselves and others. Mistakes are life's way of teaching us. We know every scratch, dent, crack, and flaw in our lives like no one else in the world possibly could. We are not expected to be perfect. Earth is a spiritual boot camp and we are supposed to fall down. If we don't fall down every once in a while; we aren't trying hard enough. Failures play an important role in our growth. We shut ourselves down by focusing on all the faults, failures, and weaknesses.

> The weak can never forgive.
> Forgiveness is the attribute of
> the strong.
> ~*Mahatma Gandhi*

We must learn from the past, let go of it, and pay attention to what is happening right now. This is where we discover new opportunities to heal past wounds. All of life's experiences serve the soul's growth and development. There are no wrong decisions, only difficult ones. How will we know our limits without an occasional failure? Higher awareness is the key where we transform any limiting negative event into a learning experience bringing confidence, clarity, and wisdom. Forgiveness is the highest form of letting go of resentment, guilt, and pain.

It is important to note that abusive relationships are destructive emotionally, physically, and spiritually. *We are better off being with no one than with the wrong one.* Small-minded people with big egos are immature souls who confuse kindness and compassion with weakness and vulnerability. No one is here to be a doormat.

Jesus, Buddha, and the other master teachers are perfect examples of unconditional love and forgiveness. They guide and inspire us to follow their example, showing that we too can make a difference in the world. We learn how love depends on our willingness to give, rather than the desire to receive. We claim our divinity by expressing unconditional love, compassion, and forgiveness.

Just as a pebble dropped in a pond creates ripples flowing outward in ever-expanding circles, so do acts of kindness and forgiveness radiate ripples of healing out to the world. We discover our true potential in life by engaging in acts kindness, compassion, forgiveness and gratitude. Life is too short to entertain negative thoughts and feelings. We need to laugh easily, love deeply, and forgive quickly. We can't change our past, but through forgiveness we can change our future.

> To forgive is to set a prisoner
> free and discover the prisoner
> was you.
> ~Lewis B. Smedes

Chapter 10
Destiny and Freewill

Destiny is no matter of chance.
It is a matter of choice. It is not
a thing to be waited for, it is a
thing to be achieved...
~*William Jennings Bryan*

There is much confusion concerning destiny and freewill. How can we have freewill if we have a destiny? What good is having freewill if we are predestined to be one thing or another? On the surface it appears destiny cancels out freewill but they are not opposing forces. All souls come to Earth with freewill and a wide variety of destinies.

We have the power to change our destiny by exercising our freedom of choice wisely. We are free to create a life where anything can and will happen depending on our thoughts, intentions, and efforts. It is our mission to move from our lowest destiny to our highest destiny in each life. Consciously we don't remember what these destinies are but on the higher levels of awareness we do. There are many different paths we can take between birth and death; the choice is ours.

Every time we use our freewill proactively and take steps necessary to change unpleasant and difficult situations in our lives, we change our destiny. Without freewill our lives would be meaningless. There would be no point to all the challenges. The whole purpose of freewill is having the freedom to choose which paths to take on our journey through life. We co-create our lives with our choices and decisions. This is not necessarily making right choices over wrong, but making better choices. This is how we learn that each choice has its consequences.

Since we were given freewill first, we are destined to make mistakes on our journey through life; it is an important part of life because our souls benefit when we learn from our mistakes. If we don't learn from our mistakes we are doomed to repeat them. Wisdom is a by-product of freewill. Mistakes are lessons in wisdom if we learn from them.

By exercising our freewill wisely, we have the power to change our destiny from chaos to fulfillment. We are born with all the powers, abilities, and tools we need to transform our lives. We can't change the past. Our upbringing may influence who we *are*, but we are responsible for who we *become*.

Life is like going to a multiplex cinema with different movies from which to choose; each is our lives. All have a beginning, middle, and an end.

In movie number one, you start drinking when you are

sixteen years old. By the time you are twenty you have given all your power away to alcohol and become an alcoholic. Everything you do at work and at home is falling apart; your life is in total chaos. One day you get disgusted with yourself and you quit drinking.

You just moved from movie number one into movie number two. You have the same beginning and the same cast of characters, but the main characters in the first movie — your drinking buddies — are only bit players; you are not hanging around with them anymore. You changed your destiny because in movie number one you were destined to die in drunken automobile accident at twenty two.

Now you are clean, sober, and thinking clearly for the first time in years, however you feel terrible physically because you have never taken care of yourself properly. You decide to start eating right and exercising. You join a health club. You focus your energy and efforts on working out and improving your health. You just moved from movie number two into movie number three. Again, your destiny is changed.

In the second movie you were destined to die of a heart attack at thirty. Now because you are eating right and exercising, it's not going to happen. In movie number three you are thinking clearly and feeling terrific but you live in the run-down part of town and you are always broke. You are living hand to mouth and tired of working at a dead-end minimum-wage job. You go back to school to learn a trade and improve your financial situation. You just moved into movie number four. Once more your destiny has changed.

In the fourth movie, you have an education, get a

much better job, and become financially independent. You have a beautiful home in an affluent neighborhood. The chaos in your life has been replaced with fulfillment, happiness, and peace of mind. You have free time to volunteer your services to help others who have given away their power to alcohol. Some of the best alcohol counselors are recovering alcoholics. Only one who knows the dark side of alcohol can look at another who is lost in the darkness and say, "I know how you feel and I know how to help you. I can show you the way out."

This is what Earth School is all about. Before we can save the world, we must save ourselves. When we save ourselves we help save the world because we are at our best. We benefit by making wiser choices and decisions. Everyone around us benefits.

We have freewill to choose which movie we want to see. When we feel boredom, depression, or a sense of pointlessness it's time for you to change movies. The movie we choose tells its own unique story. We have freewill to switch to another movie anytime we want. If we want to find out where we are now we need to reconstruct where we have been. We can change our stories, our lives, and our destiny.

> Whatever you can do, or dream
> you can do, begin it. Boldness
> has genius, power and magic in
> it.
> ~ *Goethe*

Divine Power is the electricity and we are the lamps.

We have to turn the lamp on to access the light; if we don't we are choosing to live in darkness. The Divine Power is always there waiting for us to use, but we must first take action to get the energy flowing. God transforms the world through us, not for us.

For Every Obstacle, There Are Choices

Fate does not mean that a certain situation has to turn out a particular way. Every time we face a problem or an obstacle in life we have a choice. If we choose to be reactive, filled with anger, fear, jealousy, and resentment our lives are predestined. By choosing to remain stuck in the victim role, we have decided we don't want to grow. We are sitting in the backseat of a speeding car headed for a brick wall.

On the other hand, we have the power to get into the driver's seat and take the car anywhere we want to go. With a proactive attitude we use our freewill wisely making the necessary changes required to live a rich and meaningful life.

A reactive attitude makes no transformation; it chooses to remain stuck in a life filled with pain, despair, anger and turmoil. We shouldn't let fear or frustration sabotage our potential changes. The journey is made of many small steps. When we have the courage and strength to follow our dreams, we find fear becomes less important. With one small step at a time we can create a wonderful new life story. It's not too late to change.

No matter what life brings our way, it is important to remember our happiness or sadness does not reflect either rewards or punishments from the Creator. We are the masters of our destiny because we have the freedom of choice. Life can be heaven or it can be hell depending on our thoughts and actions. Because we were given freewill before we gain wisdom we are destined to make mistakes. As long as we accept responsibility for them, they serve our soul.

Every experience in life, especially the darkest ones, is a good experience as long as we learn from it. The only bad experiences are the ones from which we fail to learn. We can use every painful situation we experience to grow. We need to make essential changes not lame excuses. Pain gets our attention by challenging the ego to surrender control. This opens the door to the healing power of the Higher Self.

> We count our miseries carefully
> and accept our blessings with-
> out much thought.
> ~ *Chinese proverb*

We are not victims; we chose to be put in situations that test how we will react to certain events in life. Our conscious mind forgets these are choices *we made* for the spiritual lessons they provide us. We — not some malevolent outer force — are responsible for everything.

Everyone is born with a unique gift to be shared with the rest of us. We must do our personal best, but avoid making everything a competition. We experience joy when we share the best we have with others and receive what they give with gratitude. We can achieve anything we desire in life. The universe will support us in our desire to complete life's greater plan. Recognize the challenges as learning opportunities. Ask for guidance and direction. Through wisdom we remember who we truly are and let go of what we are not.

> Our prayers are answered not when we are given what we ask, but when we are challenged to be what we can be.
> ~Morris Adler

Everyone comes to Earth for a reason. There is a life plan for each of us that include the most challenging situations we face in life. Nothing is left to chance. We need to look inside for life's meaning, to discover the hidden doorways that are open for us. Self-knowledge is a great power to help us achieve anything we desire in life. We must live by choice not by chance. We need only to stop, be still, and tune in to our Higher Self; it will guide us to our highest good. We each have our own unique role to play including supporting each other. The universe can open doors for us but we must have to courage to walk through them.

Problems Are Opportunities

Problems and obstacles we experience are opportunities in disguise. We may not see the big picture but we can get a clearer view. Problems cannot be solved at the same level on which they were created. By rising above the conflicts and criticism, we stop the spread of negative energy, and discover ways to promote healing from this higher perspective.

We must ask ourselves, "What do I have to learn from this situation? What steps can I take to move beyond it?" We must choose self-esteem not self-pity. The solution will always include a quality like compassion, forgiveness or acceptance. Everything and every action have a purpose; it's up to us to find it. This is the path to our highest destiny.

There are numerous examples of people born with immense disadvantages who have managed to overcome them against all odds. There are some extraordinary people who were born without arms and learned how to play guitars flawlessly and others who learned to paint beautiful pictures. There are other people without legs who climb mountains and run marathons.

Helen Keller is an excellent example of someone who achieved greatness by overcoming extreme physical challenges. A childhood illness left Helen blind and deaf. By being proactive, moving forward in the face of great adversity, she became a successful teacher and not only transformed her life, but was also a profound inspiration for millions of people, not just those with disabilities. Was Helen Keller meant to have perfect health? Was she a victim or a volunteer? Would we ever have heard of Helen Keller had she not overcome these challenges? What if she got stuck in victim consciousness and never took any action?

Change is inevitable, growth is

intentional.
~*Glenda Cloud*

Mother Teresa moved to India and dedicated her life to helping the poor. She wanted to "serve the poorest of the poor and to live among them and like them." She made tremendous personal sacrifices to help bring dignity and happiness to millions of sick and poor children.

These evolved souls came here to teach us just how powerful we really are. Their inner strength overcame seemingly insurmountable adversity. It is humbling to watch them work and to be in their presence. We are all potential Mother Teresas and Helen Kellers. Our attitude makes all the difference. We can curse our ugly feet or hands, but when we see someone with no feet or no hands we understand how blessed we truly are.

> Just because a man lacks the use of his eyes doesn't mean he lacks vision...
> ~*Stevie Wonder*

We Determine Our Destiny

Life is ten percent what happens to us, and ninety percent how we respond. When we realize that everything in our life happens by design we are better able to take the appropriate action to transform each seeming problem into an opportunity. We each have our own unique lessons to learn. Our life charts are connected with everyone else's life charts in deeper ways than we realize, because we are *one*.

> Avoiding danger is no safer in
> the long run than outright expo-
> sure...life is either a daring ad-
> venture or it is nothing.
> *~Helen Keller*

Every day life opens doors of opportunities. Our destiny is ultimately defined by which ones we choose to walk through. Our attitude makes all the difference. If we let fear stop us from walking through these doorways, our lives will be limited, frustrating, and small. Without taking any risks we will never know what or who we could be. When we feel the fear and walk through the doorway anyway we discover pathways to happiness and fulfillment.

By looking at life as an adventure instead of a chore we see change as an opportunity to grow. By releasing unproductive or stagnant patterns of thinking from the past and embracing new thoughts we change our destiny. We may be guided to a new career, to travel, relocating or possibly letting go of an old relationship. With a positive attitude we bring greater freedom of expression into our lives and the lives of others.

Good days bring us happiness. Bad days bring us valuable learning experiences. Both are essential for our souls' growth and development. Problems and obstacles we face make us strong and failures keep us humble.

Every day is a good day depending on our level of awareness.

What we bring into our life is a direct reflection of what we put out. When we replace old worn-out negative beliefs and attitudes about life with positive thoughts and intentions, we stand taller, smile easier, and shine brighter. We become the best mothers, fathers, sisters or brothers, friends, neighbors, coworkers and so on.

The universe is far greater than we have the ability to imagine. We are only as limited as our level of awareness. Mother Earth is a living, breathing spaceship in a cosmic community called the Milky Way consisting of four hundred billion stars stretching one hundred thousand light years in diameter.

Behind all of the negativity and violence we have on our planet, something much larger and far more spiritually significant is happening. A shift in the collective consciousness can change humanity's destiny. If we transform collectively we will bring more light into our world. We start by transforming ourselves. Now is the time for us to awaken to our Divine Nature. When we are awake we are able to participate in shaping our destiny and the destiny of the world.

> When you are inspired by some great purpose, some extraordinary project, all your thoughts break their bonds; your mind transcends limitations, your consciousness expands in every direction, and you find yourself

> in a new great and wonderful
> world... Dormant forces, facul-
> ties and talents become alive
> and you discover yourself to be
> a greater person by far than you
> ever dreamed yourself to be...
> ~*Pantanjali*

Chapter 11
Time Control

Half our life is spent trying to
find something to do with the
time we have rushed through
life trying to save.
~*Will Rogers*

To accomplish tasks and honor responsibilities in
life we either find the time or make the time. Being at work at eight o'clock and picking up the children
by five o'clock does not mean we know how to control
time. We are given twenty-four hours a day to spend as
we wish. Most people do not understand how to properly
use their time and they squander it believing they will
live forever.

In order to control time, we need to understand it. We
live in a fast-paced 24-7 world. We often find ourselves
racing against time, playing catch-up, trying to meet
deadlines. We are constantly on the run and the clock al-

ways seems to be ticking faster and faster. Other times we grow increasingly impatient as time slows down to a crawl. Stress and anxiety come freely as we try to cram too many activities into too little time. There never seems to be enough time for what we really want in life. We will never *find* the time to do anything. If we want more time, we must *make* it.

We have all the latest technology we need to keep us connected at all times. Cell phones, the Internet, and fax machines have brought the world closer. Our technology is designed to help us multitask because society demands it. We are able to do ten things at once and be a lot more efficient. But are we gaining really? What are we actually accomplishing by multitasking? We get more things done in less time so we can get even more done. Why?

Do we really need more time to do more things? No. We have more conveniences but we have less time than before. We learned to rush but not to wait. Sometimes we plow through important decisions without taking time to think them through. We kick ourselves later and ask, "What was I thinking?" or "What made me do that?" Just because technology is moving fast does not mean that we have to make fast decisions.

We are running around either worried about the future, or regretting the past. Memories of the past and expectations for the future are so powerful they become more real than the present. We can't meet ourselves in the past or in the future. The only place we are ever really in is the Now, the present moment. There has never been a time when we were not in the present moment. In reality the present moment is all we ever really have.

Put your hand on a hot stove
for a minute, and it seems like
an hour. Sit with a pretty girl
for an hour, and it seems like a
minute. That's relativity.
~*Albert Einstein*

We spend too much energy on the past and the future. We run around in the present with our batteries half charged — not an efficient state in which to accomplish things. How can anything work properly and efficiently with batteries that are only half charged? No wonder there is chaos in our lives. Stress, anxiety, anger, and fear are the effects of trying to function with weak batteries. When our energy is low we feel run down; we are not able to make the best choices and decisions.

We can purchase a clock, but not more time, our most valuable asset. We become so concerned with adding years to our life that we fail to add life to the years. We learned how to make a living, but we forgot how to live.

How many times have you driven across town and arrived at your destination without remembering driving down certain roads to get there? You can't remember because you were thinking about fifty other things you had to do.

How many times have you eaten an entire meal without ever remembering taking one bite because you were thinking about everything else you wanted to do?

No wonder there is so much stress and anxiety. We are never in the present moment. Many people turn to alcohol and/or drugs. Why are we numbing ourselves? Because the quick fix is a lot easier than learning how to take control of our thoughts. The effects of drug and alcohol abuse are devastating. It takes only a few seconds to open wounds that will take years to heal.

To be more effective and in balance we must make the effort to change destructive behaviors. We begin to heal on all levels by controlling our thoughts about time. We must learn to embrace the present moment because it's all we really have.

We need to give ourselves permission to relax, to slow down and enjoy the journey. It's okay to take a break and smell the roses. The world will turn without us for a while. We are happier and more effective when we are rested. We don't only miss the beautiful scenery by going too fast; we also miss the sense of where we are going and why.

> A good rest is half the work.
> ~Yugoslav proverb

When we are young we rush to grow up and when we grow up, we yearn to be young again. If we are not careful we spend our life *doing* instead of *being.* In order to control time, we must remove ourselves from it. The most important appointment we have in life is with ourselves. We need to give ourselves a break and spend some time in nature to enjoy some quiet moments for reflection. This time out charges our spiritual batteries and brings higher awareness. We have to stop and sharpen the saw every once in a while to be more effective. Work smarter, not harder. Pay attention to what's really important. We can't change the past, but we can ruin the present by worrying about the future.

If we can't spend time in nature, we can sit down, close our eyes and visualize or imagine ourselves on a beautiful beach, in a mystical forest or on top of a majestic mountain. We can use our imaginations and raise our awareness. We can go anywhere we want without ever leaving our house.

Close your eyes and imagine yourself relaxing under some tall green palm trees on a lush tropical island overlooking a deserted beach. Breathe in the fresh sea air, feel the warm sunlight on your face and a cool ocean breeze blowing through your hair. See the pure white clouds floating through a bright blue sky. Relax... release... let go... Be there in your mind using all of your senses. Imagine every detail from the sound of the waves rolling on to the beach to birds singing in the distance. Let that deep sense of peace and tranquility wash over you from the top of your head to the tips of your toes.

Release the child within. Use your imagination. The more we practice visualizing and imagining, the better it gets.

We don't need to make the time to go anywhere; we need to just do it. We can take control of time by using our mind. We have everything we need within us waiting to be recognized. Be open, be still and be in the Now ... because that's all we ever really have.

> It is in the quiet that our best
> ideas occur to us. Don't make
> the mistake believing that by a

frantic kind of dashing around
you are being your most effective and efficient self. Don't as-
sume you're wasting time when
you take time out for thought.
             ~Napoleon Hill

Chapter 12
Negative Energy

The mind is its own place, and
in itself can make a Heaven of
Hell, or a Hell of Heaven…
~ *John Milton*

Bubonic Plague — often called Black Death because of the black spots that appeared on the skin
— spread across Europe between 1347 and 1352, killing
twenty-five million people. Medieval medicine had nothing to combat this dreadful disease. Government, trade,
and commerce virtually came to a halt as one third of
Europe's population fell victim to the plague. Every part
of European society was affected by the black plague and
its duration.

The church came under immense fire when prayers for
deliverance from the plague failed. Parishioners wanted to
know why their prayers were not answered and held the
church leaders accountable for not protecting the devout.

Today scientists know that the plague was caused by deadly bubonic bacteria carried by fleas found on rats. People near those rats were bitten by the fleas, and were infected by the deadly bacteria.

During the Middle Ages people didn't know these killer germs existed because they couldn't see them. The deadly bacteria were invisible to the naked eye. Eventually everyone learned the importance of proper sanitation and the plague finally ended.

Today the world is infected with another deadly invisible plague. It killed more than one hundred million people during the twentieth century alone. Unlike the deadly bacteria in the Middle Ages, which caused visible black spots on the outside of body, this killer plague is hidden inside. This invisible deadly virus is negative energy. When we pick up the morning newspaper or turn on the evening news we see and hear about the effects of negative energy. Newspapers, radio, and television bombard us with tons of primarily negative information daily. Negative energy is a modern day plague.

People today do not respect the immense destructive power of negative energy because they cannot see it. It is invisible to the naked eye. We cannot see negative energy as physical symptoms like a rash or bruise. Because all of the damage is on the inside, we feel it. It is the knot in our stomachs, the fear in our eyes, and the pain in our hearts. What we do see are the effects of negative energy. Anger, resentment, fear, and hostility are all manifestations of negative energy that infects us like a virus contaminating our body, mind, and spirit.

We wonder why there is so much pain and suffering

in the world. We wonder why children are going to school with guns to kill their teachers and classmates. Remember what happened at Columbine High School? Those two lost souls were so infected with negative energy they thought murder was a game. People are ignorant about the destructive power of negative energy because *it is invisible*.

Parents Infect Children with High Doses of Negativity

In our ignorance, we give young children ultra-violent video games to play and movies to watch. More than half the movies Hollywood produces glorify violence and foster negative stereotypes leading to emotional and spiritual numbness. Wholesale death and destruction in the entertainment industry are poisoning our culture's mindset. We need only visit our local video store to see the volume of negativity with which we are infecting ourselves.

Violence is an easy way to make a quick buck — the bottom line in the movie industry. It's not the fault of the film companies; their mission is to make money. It's our fault because *we accept violence as entertainment.*

As parents we are the ones ultimately responsible for infecting our children with intense doses of negative energy. Now is the time to take charge and regulate the amount of negative energy we expose our children to via movies and video games. We are programming young minds with seeds of negativity, which will grow over time. It's like eating junk food every day instead of balanced meals. Where there is no nutrition, there is no health. Collectively mankind will feel the effects for generations to come.

If it were six hundred fifty years ago, I would be talking about the importance of sanitation, keeping our families and our homes free from invisible germs and bacteria. Today, negative energy is a virus that destroys our ability to see life clearly; we are playing with fire. We need to wake up and learn new ways to protect our families and keep our homes free from negative energy.

The long-term effects of pain and suffering far outweigh the short-term pleasure of gratuitous violence. It is imperative we take control of the negative energy around us and our home. There are other options available; we must make wiser choices and decisions.

The Power of Negative Energy Lingers

Imagine we are walking downtown shopping and decide to take a break and have a cup of coffee at a local café. We sit down in a booth and order the coffee. In no time we begin to feel agitated, annoyed, and uncomfortable. We start to quarrel. What happened? Everything was just fine until we sat down in the booth. What changed?

This is what actually happened. The people sitting in that booth before us had a bitter argument. They left a cloud of their negative energy in the booth. A few minutes later we sat down right in it. Immediately the negative residue started to infect us like a virus. The symptoms are found in reactive words and actions.

The only way to find the limits
of the possible is by going beyond them to the impossible.
~ *Arthur C. Clarke*

World renowned Japanese scientist, Dr. Masaru
Emoto discovered that molecules of water are affected by
our thoughts, words, and feelings. He pioneered the effects of positive energy and negative energy projected
into water.

Vials of water on which thoughts of love and gratitude
were projected formed magnificent water crystals that re-
sembled beautiful snowflakes when frozen. Vials of water from the same source but on which thoughts of anger
and hatred were projected produced grossly distorted water crystals resembling disease. The difference between
the water crystals was absolutely amazing!

Consider this: Babies are about ninety percent water.
Adult human beings are about seventy percent water. If
thoughts can affect water in a vial, what do our thoughts
do to the water in our bodies?

People who hold thoughts of anger, negativity, resentment, and hatred are distorting the water molecules in their
bodies. Negative energy destroys on all levels: physical,
mental, emotional, and spiritual. Conversely, people who
hold loving thoughts of gratitude, forgiveness, and compassion enhance the water molecules in their body. Positive energy heals on all levels: body, mind, and soul. This is the
power of prayer. To find out more about Dr. Emoto and see
the amazing photographs of the water crystals read his book
"The Hidden Messages in Water."

> A loving person lives in a lov-
> ing world. A hostile person
> lives in a hostile world: every-
> one you meet is your mirror...
> ~Ken Keyes Jr.

We Control Healing Energy

Flowers do not suddenly spring up out of the ground. Flowers grow from seeds that are buried in the earth. Physical and mental illnesses do not suddenly spring up out of nowhere, either. They start with seeds that are buried inside us. Negative energy causes stress, tension, anger, fear, and resentment which are the seeds of disease. We must make every effort to kill these destructive seeds before they become physical manifestations. Every cell in our bodies is made of atoms of energy. We have the ability to control this powerful healing energy by controlling the quality of our thoughts.

We are the actors, writers, and directors of our lives. We come to earth with all the powers, abilities, and tools we need to live rich and meaningful lives.

If we could see negative energy, it would appear as a dark fog. Everyday we are exposed to negative energy in one way or another. Even if we never leave the house, negative energy has a variety of ways of entering our living space. It will cling to us like dirt; if we don't clean ourselves off, we drag all that negativity into our homes.

If we are around people who have the flu and are sneezing and coughing, we make sure that we wash our hands before we touched our loved ones or food. Negative energy is like those germs; if we don't wash it away, we expose our families to this is insidious virus. Sometimes the people closest to us are infected with negative energy. We come home to it. Alcohol and drug abuse add fuel to the fire.

Newspapers, magazines, television, and radio are very effective ways of delivering negative energy to our doorstep. The worst thing we can do is get up in the morning, have a cup of coffee, and read about all the pain and suffering that took place in the world while we were sleeping. Murder, war, hatred, greed — all the darkness of the world — and a large dose of caffeine. What a way to start the day! It's the breakfast of champions! If we have a hardy helping of negative energy as soon as we wake up, how the heck are we supposed to make it through the day?

I'm not saying we need to be like an ostrich and stick our heads in the sand. I am saying that we don't need to be doing the backstroke in a pool of negative energy every day. We need to be aware of the world around us and current events, but we do not need to watch the news every single night and wallow in it. Be in the world but not of it.

Another thing to be aware of is the type of energy being projected into the food we eat. If the person preparing the meal is angry they are projecting their negative energy into every bite of our food. We are better off skipping a meal than eating one prepared by someone injecting their anger, resentment, and negativity into our food.

On the other hand if food is prepared by someone who

is projecting love, kindness, and compassion into our food then it contains positive healing energy.

Psychic Vampires Want an Energy Injection

We all know people who drain us of positive energy every time we see them. They are called psychic vampires. They come up to us, suck out every ounce of positive energy, and then walk away fat and happy leaving us flat on the floor. They are usually some of the people closest to us.

Instead of blood, these psychic vampires are looking for an energy feed. Most of the time the vampires do not realize they are feeding on other people's energy. They are totally unaware of the effect they have on other people. Psychic vampires are people with very low batteries and they use our energy to charge them. They hook up their invisible power cable to feed off of our energy fields. Their batteries are low because they are infected with negative energy.

There are ways to protect ourselves from these energy sucking psychic vampires. We have the power to disconnect their cables.

Buddha knew how to do it. A student tested this great teacher with disrespect and insults. Every time Buddha spoke, this student responded in an arrogant fashion. After three days the student couldn't stand it anymore. He asked Buddha, "How are you able to be so kind and loving when all I've done for the past three days is insult and offend you? Each time I disrespect you, you respond to me in a loving manner. How can this be possible"?

The Buddha responded with a question of his own. "If someone offers you a gift and you do not accept that gift, to whom does that gift belong?"

This question gave the student a new insight. When someone offers us a gift of their negativity, and we refuse to accept the gift, that gift still belongs to the giver. Why would we be angry or upset over something that belonged to someone else?

What other people do and say is a projection of their world, their reality. When we are immune to negative actions and opinions of others, we are safe from falling victim to needless pain and suffering.

> Courage is not the absence of fear, but rather the judgment that something else is more important than fear...
> ~*Ambrose Redmoon*

Work Environment Can Be Pool of Negativity

People who work in law enforcement and courtrooms are surrounded with mega doses of negativity every day; they get up and dive into a whirlpool of negativity. Unless they know how to protect themselves it's impossible not to get infected. A large percentage of them turn to alcohol and drugs as a result of being exposed to high levels of negative energy. Suicide is not uncommon. Unfortunately it may be some time before mainstream society accepts the powerful spiritual tools we have available to us for protection.

People who work in hospitals, particularly the emergency room, are also exposed to high doses of negative energy. They see the effects of exposure to this dark negative energy first hand. Stabbings, gunshot wounds, fights, assaults, overdoses, attempted suicides and more. These brave souls are an inspiration for all of us as they tend to the wounded and dying on the front lines in the war on negative energy.

Countries infected with negative energy are at war with each other to this day. Fires are extinguished in one region only to flare up in another. Let us not get depressed over the seemingly impossible situation. There is hope. Each of us has the power to help save the world in our own unique ways. The first step to save the world is to save ourselves.

> Everything that irritates us about others can lead us to an understanding about ourselves...
> ~Carl Jung

Divine White Light Protects Us

Every day we shower with water to wash away invisible germs so that we don't get sick. Every day we need to shower with the Divine White Light of God to wash away the invisible negative energy that will infect us like a virus and lower our vibration frequency. Just as we receive sunlight from the sun ninety three million miles away, we receive Divine White Light from God. Although this brilliant healing Light is invisible to the human eye, it is within and around us.

The Divine White Light is our direct connection to the Creator. When we open our hearts unconditionally, we become conduits for the light bringing it into the world. We radiate this powerful healing Light from within and from without, washing away negative energy. So every day we need to shower with the Divine White Light of the Creator.

We don't necessarily see this brilliant White Light; it does not have to look like an eight by ten color glossy picture. This spiritual cleansing process is activated through prayer and meditation.

We can also protect our families, friends, and loved ones no matter where they are by sending beams of White Light from our hearts to theirs. Visualize or imagine them happy and healthy in a ball of white light surrounding them from the top of their head to the tips of their toes.

Negative Energy Can Be Changed

Every time we find ourselves feeling angry, resentful or anything negative, we should visualize a yellow box in our mind. The box can be any size, and it has a lid but no bottom. We can imagine any negative energy coming from within or around us as darkness being drawn into the box and the lid shutting.

This dark negative energy travels out through the bottom of the box and is sent to the Creator. By visualizing this process we are purging ourselves of negative energy that cannot be destroyed. But it can be changed. When we release negative energy to the immense and all-encompassing loving power of the Divine Source, it is recycled, transformed, and reintroduced to the universe as positive energy. Why a yellow box? All the colors of a rainbow have a meaning; yellow represents personal power and self-control.

Here's one way to use that self-control. At one time or another we have all been driving down the road minding our own business when all of a sudden a car comes out of nowhere, cuts us off, and drives away. We slam on the brakes narrowly avoiding an accident. Automatically we become angry and start calling this *&^%$# knucklehead every name in the book!

All of that rage welling up from inside needs to go directly into the yellow negativity box. Just open the lid and imagine all of that anger and rage being drawn into the box and then shut the lid. Cut it off and send it all to the Creator. Every time the anger raises its ugly head, we must remember we have the power to cut it off and then forgive ourselves for getting angry.

The next thing we need to do is wrap that person and their car in White Light and pray that they don't kill themselves or someone else.

Anger is our reactive nature at work. We need to cut if off and become proactive by taking charge. This is easier said than done, but it's not impossible. It is a discipline which benefits us on all levels.

I have a small yellow box outside the front door of my house. It is a reminder for me to use it before I walk in the door. I also have a small yellow box on my desk. Good thing the box is bottomless because it fills up quickly!

When we are all stressed out and getting angry because we are stuck in traffic or at the end of a long line, it's time to use the negativity box. Remember there is a reason why we are being delayed. Perhaps we are avoiding an accident or another tragic event. Think of all the people on their way to work at the World Trade Center who got stuck in traffic, or had a flat tire or missed the train on 9/11. They were not supposed to be there because it was not their time. Everything happens for a reason and anger is not going to get us home any faster. It's better to take control of our reactive nature, relax, and enjoy the ride. Remember there is something much bigger going on.

Another powerful visualization tool to use when negative thoughts suddenly appear is to simply delete them by pressing a delete button in our minds and replacing them with positive thoughts.

These simple techniques do a good job of preventing negative energy from infecting us. By using the power of thought and intention, we are being proactive by taking control of the situation and our environment.

> Watch your thoughts, for they become words. Choose your words, for they become actions. Understand your actions, for

they become habits. Study your habits, for they become your character. Develop your character, for it becomes your destiny.
~*Frank Outlaw*

Chapter 13

Meditation

The person who looks outside
dreams.
The person who looks inside
awakens.

~Carl Jung

We all know it's not easy to maintain a balanced life-style. We can quickly overload ourselves with work, family, friends, and everyday chores. Sometimes we feel overwhelmed, anxious, and burned out. No matter what we do, happiness and peace of mind seem just out of reach.

There is a powerful life-changing technique we can use to remove ourselves from the frenzy of the outer world and within minutes replace tension with a deep sense of relaxation. This hidden gateway to inner peace and tranquility is found in meditation.

Meditation is a journey of self-discovery where we access inner guidance and wisdom. We alter our state of being through meditation and awaken to our true potential. With daily practice, peaceful awareness will saturate every area of life. We need to nourish our body every day with food and nourish our soul every day with meditation.

Meditation begins the moment we turn our attention to what is taking place in the present moment, right here, right Now. Our transformation begins when we shift our consciousness away from the ego, and unite with the love and wisdom of the higher self. We begin to heal from the inside out when we awaken from the illusion of separation from the Divine Source.

Meditation is the foundation of all spiritual growth and development. It:

1. Eliminates depression, fear and anger.
2. Enhances our creativity.
3. Develops new levels of self-awareness.
4. Boosts our intelligence.
5. Transforms our state of mind.
6. Helps us become inspired and motivated.
7. Helps us become organized and efficient.
8. Eliminates stress, tension, anxiety, and the self-centered ego.
9. Helps us become self-empowered.
10. Helps us connect with our higher self.
11. Helps us see the bigger picture.
12. Connects us with Unity Consciousness, the Divine Presence.
13. Transforms our state of being.
14. Enhances our potential.
15. Makes us feel better, get stronger, and be focused.

16. Promotes healing physically, mentally and spiritually.
17. Awakens our higher levels of consciousness: Enlightenment, Samadhi, Christ consciousness, Unity consciousness, Cosmic consciousness.

We are multidimensional spiritual beings occupying physical bodies. Our souls exist in the physical world and in the spirit world simultaneously. We are actually more spirit than flesh. In order to connect with the spirit world, we must turn within.

Western religions teach us how to *pray*; Eastern religions teach how to *meditate*. Prayer is talking to God; meditation is listening to God.

Prayer in most cases is like talking to God on the phone and then hanging up before God gets to answer. Sometimes we wonder, "Does God really hear our prayers?" To open a clear line of communication with the spirit world, we must learn how to listen.

Meditation requires no special skills or abilities. We don't have to be athletes, scholars or even spiritual. All we need is the desire. Finding inner peace is especially important today. Stress and anxiety are byproducts of our fast-paced lives; they are the seeds all disease (dis-ease) mental, emotional, and physical. Alcohol and drugs are a quick fix that impacts our lives and everyone around us, especially the ones we love most. Substance abuse is like throwing gasoline on a fire; everyone gets burned.

The path to true peace and tranquility is internal; we take it everywhere we go. We can access serenity and stillness, anytime we want through meditation. With practice we can meditate in a crowded room, in a doctor's office, at work, in school, anywhere.

We can extend the length of life by only so much. With meditation, however, we can expand the size of our life two-, three- or four-fold. So, if we live for seventy-five years but we have lived twice as large in each moment, it will be like living one hundred fifty years. This is not an impossible achievement. This is something that everyone can do through meditation.

> And in the end it's not the years
> in your life that count. It's the
> life in your years...
> ~*Abraham Lincoln*

The limit of our power of perception is not the limit of all there is to perceive. There are many filters of awareness between us and the Creator, but there are no filters between the Creator and us. Through meditation, we are able to remove these filters and achieve Unity Consciousness experiencing Oneness with the Divine Source. This is a place where spiritual energy flows unobstructed, and there is no fear, negativity or separation. In sacred unity we connect with the unifying spirit of God within all of creation.

We Must Train Our Monkey Minds

Our minds are like little monkeys jumping here and there, wherever and whenever they want. Unless we tame our monkey minds they will rule our lives. Meditation is a transformative process where we train the monkeys to sit still and be quiet. It is in that still, silent space we connect in sacred awareness with the Divine Presence infusing us with a deep sense of peace and tranquility.

Meditation doesn't only benefit us when we are seated quietly. Through meditation we bring greater awareness to every activity in our life whether it is work or recreation because we are aware of the unlimited possibilities available to us.

Through meditation we temporarily shut down our five senses turning off our attention to the outer world and focusing our attention on the present moment. This gives us the ability to slowly quiet our minds. In this silence we merge our minds with God's and become aware of our connection to all things in Unity Consciousness. After all, our minds *are* God's mind.

Life takes on new dimensions through meditation transforming the ordinary into extraordinary. On the higher levels of consciousness, only love exists. Fear, doubt, and negativity cannot abide in the upper realms. We allow Unity Consciousness to flow through us effortlessly infusing us with power, freedom, and grace. Amazing things start to happen on our journey to greater self-awareness. This is the path to awakening. The person that goes in one side of the meditation experience is not the same person who comes out the other side.

Now Allows Us to Access Spirit World

We carry within us a doorway, a threshold to the spirit world, a way for human beings to access higher levels of consciousness, a way of connecting to unlimited spiritual energy. We receive it at birth but it is hidden in a place we never go... the "present moment." Even if we manage to let go of the past, and release thoughts about the future and get into today, we are still concerned about something we should have done in the morning and something we have to do at night. *We are never in the present moment*. Focusing our attention on the past and future chains us to a life of regret and fear. Meditation enables us to release the past and the future and get into the *"absolute Now."*

> Make time for the quiet moments because God whispers and the world is loud.
> *~unknown*

In the spirit world there is only eternity, timelessness. Everything we see as past, present and future is compressed into "Now time." When we focus our attention on the Now we discover our connection to the spirit world.

Meditation is the way to shut down our five senses and get into the present moment. By focusing on our breathing, we learn to release our thoughts and quiet the mind. This is a discipline well worth practicing. Don't entertain thoughts as they float into your mind. Delete them or just release them and let them float out like clouds as easily as they drifted in. Pay attention to your breath, gently flowing in and out. Breathe in peace and breathe out tension; breathe in calm and breathe out stress and anxiety. Eventually thoughts will slow down and eventually stop coming, quieting the mind.

> When I let go of what I am, I
> become what I might be.
> ~ *Lao Tzu*

In the Now we transcend space and time revealing the doorway within. As we move through that inner threshold we connect with greater awareness. We are free from worries, fears, cares, and concerns. Peace and tranquility wash over us from the top of our heads to the tips of our toes, filling every cell and every atom in your body with a radiant, healing, Divine White Light. This is the healing Light of God. It comes from the Creator the way sunlight comes from the sun. Every day we need to shower with white light to wash away negative energy the way we shower with water to wash away germs.

With our spiritual batteries charged we become self-empowered. We make better choices and decisions. Our hearts open to receive divine guidance and inspiration transforming obstacles into opportunities. Balanced and centered, we discover the sacred dimensions of every day life. In the midst of any activity or situation, we remain centered and at peace, secure in the Divine Presence of the Creator.

> Cultivate virtue, do no harm
> and tame your mind.
> ~ *Buddha*

The Mind is Like a Radio

Our minds are like radios. We tune into a variety of stations everyday. The thoughts we receive vary with the station. Our choice of stations will range from negative to positive as well as past, present, and future.

Our freewill is the dial with which we select stations; the choice is ours. However, if we relinquish control, our *egos* will choose the stations for us, and most of the time, they are negative. This is because our ego relies on our five senses for information. Our five senses give us a very limited understanding of the world and our place in it. This lack of understanding creates fear and negativity. Nothing positive ever came from negative thoughts.

Our responsibility is to maintain control over which radio stations our minds select as thoughts from the collective consciousness bombard us. We have to be aware of them and tune out anything negative.

Through meditation we learn to take control of the mind radio, and tune into the highest frequency station available. This radio station is found in the present moment, in the Now. Even Masters had to take the first step in meditation, so can you.

Expanding Aura Meditation

Sit down in a comfortable position with your back straight and close your eyes. Rest your hands in your lap with the palms facing up. Relax and focus on your breathing, through your nose. Breathe in slow and long.

Deep belly breathing. Feel the breath gently flowing in and out. Breathing in peace... breathing out tension... breathing in calm... breathing out stress and anxiety... Your body becomes relaxed and peaceful.... and your mind comes to rest. Visualize or imagine a bright white ball of light above your head shining down, all the way down to the tips of your toes. Breathe in this radiant light. See it filling your lungs and spreading out to every cell and every atom in your body until you are a radiant ball of bright, white light shining from within and without.

See it expanding out, filling the room, and everyone in the room with this radiant white light, and then see it filling the building, the property, the planet. See everyone on the planet smiling and at peace as they are bathed in this radiant, healing, divine, white light.

Repeat:
I send God's Love and Light.
I receive God's Love and Light.
I am God's Love and Light.

Expand this light out to our solar system and all the planets in the solar system, then out to fill the Milky Way Galaxy.

Repeat:
I send God's Love and Light.
I receive God's Love and Light.
I am God's Love and Light.

Feel the energy rise as you connect in consciousness with all other beings in the galaxy deep in prayer and meditation. Now expand the light out to fill the universe and all of creation in every dimension.

Repeat:
I send God's Love and Light.
I receive God's Love and Light.
I am God's Love and Light

We are conduits for the authentic power of the Creator. Feel this powerful, loving, radiant, white light healing you physically, mentally, and spiritually.

Repeat:
There is nothing God cannot do.
There is nothing God cannot do through me.
There is nothing God cannot do as me.
God and I are One.
Therefore there is nothing I cannot do.
Nothing is too good for God.
Therefore nothing is too good for me.
I am unlimited.
I am eternal.
I affirm Divine Order.
I affirm we are One.
I affirm I am going to meet my highest good.
Rest quietly in the Now…
Filled with peace and tranquility…
In communion with the Divine Presence…

Meditation illuminates the mind. Our inner vision is strengthened as we move forward with wisdom and clarity. The Divine Presence guides us to perfect understanding. We see beyond apparent limitations to the abundance of spirit and realize that all things are possible.

> Only in quiet waters things mirror themselves undistorted. Only in a quiet mind is adequate perception of the world.
> ~Hans Margolius

Chapter 14

Spirit Guides & Guardian Angels

He who knows others is wise,
he who knows himself is
Enlightened.
~*Lao Tzu*

All souls who come to Earth have Spirit Guides. These compassionate souls have chosen to stay here and help guide others on the path to spiritual awakening. They are advanced souls who have completed their incarnations on Earth and work as our personal guides and teachers. Our guides are spiritual coaches who help us to be our best, learn our lessons, and complete our many tasks. In Buddhism these compassionate beings are called Bodhisattvas dedicated to helping all conscience beings reach enlightenment.

Life on Earth is severe; we can use all the support and guidance we can get from our invisible best friends. Spirit Guides have experienced the instincts, emotions, and desires along with a deep-rooted sense of isolation and fear programmed into human beings. There are many challenges for a soul occupying a human body on this planet. This is why only the *most courageous souls* volunteer to incarnate on Earth.

We have one "Master Guide" that stays with us from birth to death. We also have a number of secondary Spirit Guides that come and go depending on our ever-changing needs as we journey through life. Our needs at ten years old are different than at thirty which are different than at sixty. Through prayer and meditation we are able to connect with our spiritual guides and develop a relationship with them. We can ask them for assistance to help us complete our lessons. They want what's best for us but they cannot do the work for us. They cannot tell us what to do because that would cancel out our freewill. Our guides show us signs and inspire us to move in the right direction. It is in our best interest to follow our intuition.

Our relationship with our guides is student and teacher rather than parent and child. The more mature the student is, the more advanced the Spirit Guide assigned to them is.

Along the way our guides watch us make mistakes that are painful not only for us, but for them as well. They are compassionate souls that support us during times of grief, sorrow and despair. Their teaching methods differ depending on the level of our soul's maturity. Our guides help us learn lessons and complete our spiritual mission. They help us restore balance and act as healers.

Synchronicities Are Flags to Get Our Attention

Synchronicity is the experience of two or more events which occur in a meaningful manner. Spirit Guides create these meaningful coincidences to get our attention. People, places, and events are guided into our life to help us place emphasis on what we are experiencing and to reach higher levels of awareness.

Synchronicities are signal flags in life that say, "Take another look; there is something much bigger going on here." Pay attention. These odd experiences have a deeper meaning. They are not random accidents or coincidences.

Synchronicities are parallel occurrences that are connected in mysterious ways. They move us beyond normal borders and boundaries. They can pull together very different people for a common purpose, which can bring about physical, emotional, and spiritual healing. Special people appear in our lives at key moments. When the student is ready, the teacher appears. When we are aware, synchronicities can give us guidance and insight, helping us make better choices and decisions.

Uncommon, extraordinary events happen by design to get us to sit up and take notice. Perhaps one wakes up every night at the same time, or every time one looks at the clock it says 2:22, 3:33, 4:44 or 11:11 etc. Receiving a phone call or a letter from someone we haven't heard from in a long time just as we were thinking about them is another synchronicity. Our Spirit Guides use synchronicities to help us achieve the goals and learn the lessons that were written into our life charts.

Secondary Spirit Guides come into our lives with a specific purpose to help us complete specific tasks. Writers or artists might call on a Spirit Guide for creative inspiration. A doctor or nurse might call on a Spirit Guide to assist in healing. Spirit Guides are our constant companions. (The next time you need a good parking spot, ask your Spirit Guide for assistance. You will be amazed how often you get one in front of the entrance!)

Our Spirit Guides have Spirit Guides watching over them from the upper realms. Their skills as guides and teachers are being monitored by highly evolved beings. One day when we complete our incarnations we may choose to stay on as Spirit Guides or Bodhisattvas.

Angels Protect, Guide Us

We also have Guardian Angels who are here to protect us. Angels are the "Messengers of God" who seek only to fulfill the will of the Creator. Angels are Beings of Light who appear in human form as either male or female, but are neither; they are androgynous along with all spiritual beings including us.

Angels are higher up on the spiritual ladder and closer to the Creator than Spirit Guides; they do not work with one person exclusively. They have never incarnated and do not know what it's like to be human although they have been known to take human form to accomplish specific tasks. Guardian Angels are compelled to work on our behalf throughout our lives; all we have to do is call them.

Our Spirit Guides and Guardian Angels were the last ones we saw before we incarnated and they will be the first ones we meet when we return home to the spirit world.

We meet our Spirit Guides and Guardian Angels through *meditation*. They bring insight and information. Our guides will work with us in a way we understand. Spirit Guides and Guardian Angels work differently with each student in their care. They know our individual strengths and weaknesses and guide us accordingly. They speak to us telepathically and with practice, we can learn how to listen to their voices. Many of the thoughts we have are generated by our Spirit Guides.

Thomas Appears As My Spirit Guide

About the time I became an altar boy, I began receiving communications telepathically from spiritual beings, although I did not know it at the time. At first I thought perhaps the voice I was hearing was a figment of my imagination, something I was making up.

As a young boy in Catholic school I learned that everyone has a Guardian Angel. I thought perhaps that was the voice in my head. My teachers at school did not elaborate about how Guardian Angels communicate with us. I just knew I was being watched over by someone I could not see with my eyes. I never told anyone about my experiences because I didn't want anyone to think there was something wrong with me.

It was at this time I volunteered to become an altar

boy. I remember serving my very first Mass. My feet never touched the ground. I will never forget that feeling. It was a sign I was headed in the right direction spiritually; my relationship with God grew even stronger.

I didn't verbalize my feelings, but I did volunteer to serve Mass more often. Some Sundays I served twice. I especially enjoyed serving Mass for the nuns in their convent chapel at 6 a.m. (although my father may not have been thrilled about getting up early to drive me there). I had a special relationship with the nuns who were my teachers at school. They were strict disciplinarians but always treated me with kindness. It was at this time I found the coin on the beach and it changed my life. I knew God was watching over me. In my mind there was never a doubt.

As I grew older I asked deeper questions about the spirit world. They were inadequately answered and left me feeling empty. I became disenchanted with the Catholic Church. I was inspired to look beyond the walls of fear, guilt and dogma that surrounded me. I explored other ancient traditions of the world including Buddhism, Hinduism, Judaism, and early Christianity which I discovered is filled with mysticism. I learned we have Guardian Angels and Spirit Guides.

I was ready when my teacher appeared. It was at this time that I met my spiritual mentor, Michelle Gellman. She taught me how to develop my spiritual powers and abilities through meditation.

One day, while meditating a familiar voice began speaking to me telepathically. I listened for a minute or two and asked who it was.

"You can call me Thomas."

"Well, Thomas, how do I know you are real? How do I know I am not just making this up in my head?"

"What is it you want me to do to prove to you I am real?"

I thought for a moment, and said, "If you are real Thomas, I want you to show me a dove...not just a dove, but a pure white dove...no black spots, no gray feathers, only a pure white dove."

"So be it."

A short time later I ended the meditation. When it was over, I had the strong desire to listen to a song I had not heard in years. I knew I had it in my music collection, but I didn't know exactly where it was filed. I went to the section where I thought it might be and began pulling back a row of music filed in alphabetical order. When I looked down at the picture on the front of the album cover I saw it — a picture of a pure white dove held in the hands of a naked Black man. I was absolutely stunned!

I couldn't believe how fast it happened. I was like a child on Christmas Eve. I couldn't wait to meditate the next day. Halfway through the meditation Thomas appeared. I said to him, "That was really good Thomas; I am very impressed...but it all happened so fast. I need another validation; I just want to be sure this is real."

Thomas asked me what I wanted him to do this time.

"I want someone to bring a single red rose into my house. Not a picture of a rose, not an artificial rose, not a dozen roses, but a single red rose."

"It is done."

I came out of the meditation and went on with my day. I meditated every day that week without hearing a single word from Thomas. By the seventh day I had all but forgotten about the red rose validation I requested.

When my sister Debra and her family came to visit, I opened the front door and she handed me a beautiful bouquet of white carnations. I looked down at the flowers and discovered the carnations were surrounding a single red rose. I was dazed!

I was so excited I went around showing everyone the flowers, and telling them to remember the red rose. Everyone was wondering why I was making such a big deal about a red rose. I was on cloud nine the whole day!

I asked my sister why she brought flowers (which she had *never* done before). She said this bouquet caught her eye at the store and thought they would be a nice gift.

She was right; it was a gift I will remember for the rest of my life. Once again I was a child on Christmas Eve anxious to meditate the next day.

The following day while meditating, Thomas appeared. "Was seven days long enough?"

"Yes, it was definitely long enough Thomas. You have my undivided attention. What is it that you want from me?"

Thomas explained he was my Spirit guide here to help me stay on the path and achieve my spiritual goals. Having no idea what my spiritual goals were at that time, I could use all the help I could get.

Thomas did not disappoint me. Over the next few months, I was guided to some very special teachers in this world and on the other side who helped me hone my skills in spirit communication. This was a major turning point in my life.

I have since met other "secondary" Spirit Guides who work with me along with Thomas my Master Guide, and Maria, my Guardian Angel. I know there are others I have yet to meet. It is comforting to know we have a kind, compassionate, and very patient spiritual support team we can rely on for guidance and protection on our journey through life.

> There comes that mysterious meeting in life when someone acknowledges what we are and what we can be, igniting the circuits of our highest potential.
> ~*Rusty Berkus*

Chapter 15
Death

Learn like you'll live forever,
live like you'll die tomorrow.
~*Mahatma Gandhi*

For most of us death isn't real until someone we love dies. All of a sudden we start asking important questions:

- Is there life after death?
- Have our loved ones gone to a better place?
- What is the meaning of life?

Why wait for someone close to us to die or a terminal illness to shock us into examining life and death? Ignoring the reality of dying is the main reason we have so much difficulty facing death.

Our culture has made many great technological advances but virtually none spiritually. Driven by consumerism we became lost in the material world. We have no real understanding of death and the significant role it plays. We spend more time and money keeping our bodies beautiful while completely ignoring our souls.

There is much fear and misunderstanding about death because we have lost track of our priorities. Many people are in denial of death; they think by ignoring death it will go away. They fail to realize the only reason we come to earth is for spiritual growth and development. They live in ignorance and indifference of all that is sacred. Death is perceived by many others as a final end.

Death is the least-understood universal experience. It is perfectly natural to fear death; we naturally fear what we don't understand. We must make the time while we are alive and well to learn about the important role death plays in life. Death is a valued teacher that brings us face to face with the immortality of our souls. Everyone dies, but everyone does not truly live.

Death challenges us not to waste time. Don't get lost chasing after material possessions. Money can be replaced, time can't. Lost time with loved ones can never be recovered. We must cherish our relationships, not our possessions. Now is the time to express love to those close to us. Life is change and nothing we love should ever be taken for granted.

We Need to Grieve for Those We Lose

When a loved one dies we honor their life through grief. It's important to allow ourselves to grieve; it is the first step on the road to healing. We should speak to the departed from the heart and send them blessings; they can hear us. When we focus on the wisdom gained through this relationship we realize our time together was a gift, a precious opportunity to learn about love and forgiveness. This gives our relationship with them meaning and makes our life richer. There are no losses, only blessings. Keep in mind our loved ones are not only well again, they are young again. They are reunited with family, friends, and beloved pets that passed before them. Our relationships with loved ones on the other side have not ended; they have evolved because *love is stronger than death*.

Nature Separates, Spirit Unites

All things have spirits including plants and animals. People with green thumbs connect with the spirit of plants. Their relationship with each other is more than good fertilizer and fresh water. Native Americans use plants and herbs in their sacred rituals blending the spirit of the plants with their spirits.

The best veterinarians and animal trainers connect with the spirits of animals. They communicate on a soul level with the animals. When a beloved pet passes away our loved ones on the other side are there to take the pets' spirit home to our circle of love. Pets give and receive love unconditionally. They teach us about love, loyalty and commitment. Spirits come through with their pets in my readings all the time. Nature separates us from the animal kingdom, but our love unites us with them in spirit.

Wild animals on the other hand, have group souls. At death the spirit of a wild animal returns to the group soul of hawk, buffalo, tiger, dolphin etc. Don't listen to anyone or organization that tells you animals do not have souls. That is a cruel lie.

Birth and death are not opposites. They are part of a cycle the same as sunrise and sunset. Death is just another chapter in the book of life. Death is essential; it gives life its deepest reality.

Death has many facets:

1. Life and death are one.
2. We leave the earth school and return home to the spirit world through the portals of death.
3. Our relationships with loved ones continue after death.
4. Heaven and hell are states of mind, not physical locations of rewards and punishment.
5. There is no fear or guilt in the spirit world.
6. The basic truths of death are understandable.
7. We are spiritual beings in physical bodies, not physical bodies with spirits.

Terminally Ill Have Heightened Awareness

Terminally ill patients facing death journey through grief, anger, acceptance, and eventually surrender. Many of them speak openly and honestly about death with a heightened sense of awareness. This enables them to express a deep appreciation for the simple things in life. Trivia no longer matters. Their perspective grows and they live moment to moment at a deeper level. They are in many ways more alive now while facing death than they were before.

The fragrance of a flower, a beautiful sunset, a child's laughter confirms there is something much greater going on. Nothing is ordinary; everything's extraordinary. Each moment they have with a loved one is precious because their time is so short. There is no time for pettiness. A kind word, gentle touch, and even the smallest act of compassion is true wealth.

Death teaches us life is a priceless gift because our time here is limited. Living without the awareness of death makes it harder to appreciate the wonder and beauty surrounding us. We develop habits that stall growth and block our awareness. We easily fall into complacency and overlook our many blessings. Too often we fail to recognize precious opportunities life offers us. Somewhere along the way we lose perspective of what gives life meaning. If we are not aware, we get caught up in the superficial illusions and pointless dramas of the material world.

There are many people with grave illnesses struggling to bring spirituality into their life for the first time. They come in two categories.

- People who look to the past. They are filled with regrets because they realize their unkind words and actions.

- People who look to the future. They start promising God anything if they are healed. "I promise I'll do anything you want Oh Lord, if you cure me now." These are what combat soldier's call Foxhole prayers.

Why wait until a crisis hits? Don't look back with regret or forward with fear. We discover our connection to the Divine Presence of the Creator in the present moment. Tomorrow is promised to no one. We must live our faith today, not in the past or in the future. Today is the day to make a difference, use kind words and actions, turn the other cheek with forgiveness and help one another.

Higher awareness is the key that provides spiritual power and freedom. Power to achieve things we never dreamed possible is within each of us. We are divine beings with unlimited potential. Our heritage is sacred. Now is the time to use our divine inheritance to bring deeper meaning to our lives and those around us.

> Wisdom is doing those things living that are desired when dying.
> ~ *unknown*

Take a Good Look at Life to the Present

Every now and then we should go through a life review. We should lie down, close our eyes, and pretend it is our last day on earth. Examining our lives from that perspective is a cleansing process that strips away all nonessentials and exposes the soul. New insights to life will begin to emerge as we let more light in. We need to ask ourselves:

- What are my priorities?
- What do I need to let go?
- What would I miss the most?
- How well am I using my time?
- What habits do I have to change?
- How can I serve others?

We need to look for paths that will give life meaning. Ask forgiveness for everyone who has ever crossed us; forgive ourselves. We are supposed to make mistakes on our journey through life so we can learn from them.

During the life review process we will discover the courage to face our deepest fears. Fear keeps us from living our true potential. We can't let fear stop us. Fear blocks the light. Nothing in life is to be feared; it is only to be understood. Fears disappear when we have the courage to face them. The main danger is taking too many precautions. The brave don't live forever; the frightened don't live at all. Life is meant to be spent not saved.

> As a well spent day brings
> happy sleep, so life well used
> brings happy death.
> ~Leonardo da Vinci

Living each day as though it's the last one keeps us grounded in the present moment. Learn from the past, look to the future, but live in the Now. Why cry over words left unsaid and deeds left undone? The most important thing we can know at death is that our life had meaning. Now is the time to give life meaning.

> When I stand before God at the
> end of my life, I would hope that
> I would not have a single bit of
> talent left, and could say, 'I used
> everything you gave me.'
> *~Erma Bombeck*

We are busier than ever and can easily lose sight of our true priorities. We come here to add what we can to life, not take from it. Most people focus on their financial bank accounts and completely ignore their spiritual bank accounts. Their priorities are placed on self-esteem not self-worth.

Which bank account means the most when we die? We can't take a penny with us at death. All we can take are the spiritual deposits we made in life through acts of kindness, compassion, charity, and forgiveness. These are the only investments that never fail.

> Life is not measured by the
> number of breaths we take, but
> by the moments that take our
> breath away.
> *~ Hilary Cooper*

Death reminds us that we must think deeply about our relationships and our values. If we are not careful we get lost. It is easy to get sidetracked in the material world. Joy is not found in material things, it is found within us. It is our responsibility to keep track of our motivations, and habits while making every effort to pass our spiritual classes at the Earth School. If we don't we will have to come back here and take these same exact classes all over again. Why repeat the same classes?

If We Inhabit the Earth Our Work Is Not Done

As long as we are alive our work on Earth is not done. The true value of death is to call attention to the present moment. No one leaves here one second before or after they are supposed to, except through suicide. Suicide is never written in our life contract.

We are immortal spiritual beings occupying a wide variety of physical bodies on our journey through eternity. We are born with immense spiritual power woven into the fabric of our being. Kindness, compassion, wisdom, joy, and peace are our divine inheritance. We have no fear of death when we understand the important role it plays in life. Human birth is hard to attain. We must use this precious opportunity to do something of value.

Everyone is equal in death's presence. When we return home to the spirit world, it is not the medals, money, or diplomas that matter. It is all the scratches, dents, and scars that mean the most. We are not supposed to go home all pretty and neat because that means we didn't try hard enough in life. We must use our time on Earth wisely by showing kindness, compassion, and forgiveness to others today.

At death the Grim Reaper transforms into a beautiful Angel of Light radiating unconditional love and compassion that comes to guide us back home where we wake up and realize we were *never away from home* at all.

Death holds no fear for me;
for my soul is eternal,
never ceasing to be.
My soul is like the sun, which
from my earthbound point of view
seems to set each night,
but actually never does.
~Anonymous

Chapter 16
Near Death Experience

All we have to decide is what
to do with the time we are
given.

~Gandalf

A large number of people have had near-death experiences (NDEs). They were clinically dead for a short period of time after an accident, a heart attack, during surgery or some other event and then came back to life. One out of five people report near-death experiences.

Each said at first they floated a few feet over their body, looking down with a feeling of detachment. They observed everyone standing around, heard everything the people were saying, and began to rise even higher.

Next they traveled through a tunnel with a bright white light off in the distance beckoning to them. As each approached the radiant white light they were completely overcome with an overpowering feeling of pure love and joy a billion times greater than is humanly possible. Waves of this intense powerful loving, joyful, healing energy vibrated in and around them.

A deceased family member or Being of Light was standing in this radiant loving light. Feelings of peace and tranquility washed over them as this person or being approached. Unity and *oneness* prevailed. Some of the NDEs report going through a life review at this point and they were shown areas in their lives that needed attention.

Then to their dismay, they were told telepathically they could not stay. Their work was not finished and they had to return to earth. No matter how much money they had, or family they had, or how much they had to live for, none of them, *not a single one*, wanted to come back to Earth. That's how magnificent home is.

The next thing they knew they were rapidly moving through the tunnel and back into their bodies. The experience left them all with intense feelings of unconditional love and compassion for all living things. They lost all fear of death. On top of that, every one of them had heightened psychic abilities. Their ultimate message is that life is precious and profoundly meaningful and that we are One. We are all individual expressions of the Divine Source.

Following are a couple of examples of NDEs.

Carl Finds True Wealth

Carl was a stressed-out, overworked corporate executive. His job took a toll on his heart and he had bypass surgery. In the middle of the operation Carl had a near-death experience. The first thing he remembered was floating over his body near the ceiling looking down at the doctors and nurses desperately trying to revive him; he had flat-lined. He hovered overhead for a minute and then floated out of the operating room, down a long hallway to the waiting room where he saw his wife and family praying for him.

The next thing Carl knew he was moving rapidly through a long dark tunnel with a blissful bright white light at the end pulling him toward it. As he entered the light he was filled with an intense, pulsating, radiating, surge of pure love, joy, and peace beyond measure. Suddenly a magnificent, loving Angel or Being of Light appeared in front of him and told him that he could not stay; it was not his time and he had to return to Earth.

Carl adamantly told the Angel there was no way he was leaving. He was determined to stay in this blissful, loving place.

The Angel told him his work on earth was not finished. Being a man of his word, he could not leave until his work was completed. Carl knew he had to return finish the greater work.

The next thing Carl knew he was being pulled backward through the tunnel away from the light and back into his body with a jolt. He could see his heart bleeping on the EKG monitor as the doctors and nurses began cheering. The next day he woke up in the critical care unit a totally new man. He not only lost all fear of death, he was actually looking forward to it! He made the decision to dedicate his life to helping underprivileged children. A short time later Carl was back on its feet.

The first thing he did was walk into his boss's office and quit his job; there was more to life than making money and Carl had something more important to do. Carl was raised in an orphanage and he worked very hard to make his way in the world. Life is tough enough when you do have a family to support you; it's extra hard when you're an underprivileged orphan. He started an organization for underprivileged children to help them find their way in the world, to give them the opportunity to live rich and meaningful lives.

Carl has never been happier in his life. He learned true wealth isn't seen with the eyes, it is felt with the heart.

Dog, Grandmother Greet Rose on Other Side

Rose was a teenager who nearly drowned. From above she saw her lifeless body lying at the bottom of the pool. People were yelling to call a doctor as she watched them pull her limp, lifeless body out of the water. They were desperately trying to resuscitate her; she didn't understand why everyone was making such a fuss. Immediately she was emotionally detached from the situation.

She felt herself traveling through a long, dark tunnel with a bright light at the end. As she approached this radiant, loving, bright white light, her pet dog, who had died years ago came running out to greet her and guide her into the light. Overcome with joy at seeing her beloved pet alive and well, Rose followed the dog into the light and suddenly her deceased grandmother appeared.

Her grandmother was beautiful with a radiant white

light glowing all around her. She told Rose she was going to be the mother of three beautiful children and she had to return to her earthly body. Still Rose did not want to leave and went to pick up her dog. Her grandmother stopped her and said "No not now, this is not your time" then she smiled, and waved good-bye. All of a sudden Rose felt herself traveling back down through the tunnel.

The next thing Rose knew she was back in her body gasping for air. At first she was disappointed she couldn't stay with her grandmother on the other side. As time went by Rose knew that when it was her time to go home they would one day meet again. She continued to have psychic experiences including visits from her grandmother.

Years later she married and became the mother of three beautiful children.

Wormhole Connects Physical, Spiritual Worlds

The long tunnel with a bright white light at the end is a wormhole which connects the physical world to the spirit world. It is a portal, a passageway we travel through at birth and death that connects the various dimensions. When we die and step out of the physical body we go right into the astral plane.

This is where the tunnel and the light connect with the physical universe. If we turn away from the light we are stuck in the fourth dimension. The light is always available to us but we must want to go there. We are not forced into the light; but hanging around the astral plane is like going to Disneyland and staying in the parking lot instead of going into the park.

Not all near-death experiences are the same. Some people report seeing nothing at all before returning to life while others report having an unpleasant experience. The ones who had the most frightening experiences were usually people with a deep belief in a final judgment with punishing tribunals filled with fire and brimstone or they were people with no belief system. These people describe time spent in the astral plane with either a Spirit Guide or souls who did not return to the light. We are all on our own unique spiritual journeys; our experiences are guided by our beliefs.

Christians would report seeing Jesus rather than Buddha and Hindus would report seeing Krishna rather than Moses. These religious figures are archetypes we relate to. Most people who have a NDE don't report seeing religious figures; they report seeing deceased family members, Angels or Beings of Light.

Our experiences at death vary depending on how spiritually evolved we are. Mature souls are less likely to be greeted by a family member and go directly home because they know their way.

> You must 'be the change' you
> wish to see in the world.
> ~*Mahatma Gandhi*

Chapter 17
Alzheimer's, Dementia & Coma

The people who make a difference in your life are not the
ones with the most credentials,
the most money, or the most
awards. They are the ones that
care.

~Charles Schultz

Before birth the soul fuses with a fetus in the
mother's womb. The soul enters the physical
body through the top of the head. This spiritual doorway
is called the "Crown Chakra." When the soul leaves the
physical body at death it exits out through the Crown
Chakra and returns home.

For people with Alzheimer's, dementia, Parkinson's
and other long-term debilitating diseases or those in a
coma, the soul is slowly "leaking" out of the physical
body through the top of the head. The soul leaves little by

little over a long period time.

Most of their spiritual energy is floating over their physical bodies. They see everything that is being done and hear everything being said. It is important to stay positive when you are around them.

The Spirits do not have to stay with the physical body. They come and go as they please. I have done many readings were someone has come through with other family members on the other side while their physical body was in a nursing home many miles away. Their soul is still connected to the body, but because they are mostly outside of it they're not stuck in one location. At death the last one percent of his/her spiritual energy slips out of our bodies through the top of our heads and we are home.

People with Alzheimer's, which is growing to epidemic proportions, are already home with their loved ones on the other side. They were home in spirit before they left their physical bodies. They happily talk to deceased family and friends who are in the room with them while the caregiver nervously looks around the empty room.

There are spirits around us all the time; always have been, always will be. Just because we can't see or hear them doesn't mean they aren't standing right next to us. If we had special glasses that could see all the spirits that are around us all our fears would fade away.

When our souls slowly start to leave the dense, heavy, physical body at death, our energy frequency begins to rise. The higher our vibrations rise the easier it is for us to see and hear the nonphysical beings in the spirit realm. Remember, everything is energy and the spirit world's frequency is outside our range of reception.

They are not watching you do the dishes or laundry. They have more important things to do in the spirit world. However they are here at key moments to support, guide, and protect us.

This also happens with all people who are slowly leaving their physical bodies no matter what disease they have. Many of my clients were caregivers who sat by a loved one's bedside looking around the empty room while the patient is happily chatting with a roomful of invisible people. Our loved ones in spirit know when we are going to cross over and often come to meet us and guide us home, whether it is through long-term illness or a sudden unexpected death.

I have heard many amazing stories involving this subject. Following are a couple of them as well as one of my own experiences.

Ernie Helps Grandma Communicate

Jay lost his best friend Ernie in a car accident. They had served in the Marines together and were like brothers watching over each other in combat. Not being a man of faith, Ernie's untimely death weighed heavily upon Jay.

A few months after the accident Jay, who lives in Florida, received a phone call from his grandmother in New York. She told Jay that his friend Ernie was in the room with her and asked her to call him. His grandmother described Ernie perfectly —height, build, facial features everything right down to a scar on his face and his short blonde hair. Ernie wanted to say hello and let Jay know he was okay and watching over him.

Jay stood there with the phone in his hand and his mouth wide open in total shock. Not only because his deceased friend Ernie visited his grandmother, but also because his grandmother was totally blind and in the late stages of Alzheimer's! She couldn't remember Jays name let alone his phone number, or even how to use a phone. Grandma was lucid and spoke clearly; she hadn't done that in years. Once Jay gained his composure he called his mother to tell her what happened; to this day no one in his family believes him.

Jay's grandmother was able to see and hear Ernie clearly because most of her spiritual energy was out of her body. Ernie helped Jay's grandmother get back into her body, dial the phone, and deliver the message.

> Everyone is God in disguise...
> Let no one ever come to you
> without leaving better and happier.
> ~*Mother Teresa*

Steve's Grandma Talks with Deceased Relatives

Steve's grandmother sat straight up in her deathbed and had a conversation with her daughter Lily. No one had told grandma that Lily had died in a car accident two weeks earlier because her health was too fragile.

Steve was in shock as he looked around the room

wondering what the heck was going on. Then grandma started talking to her deceased husband, Bill, who had come with Lily. After a minute or two, a beautiful smile came across grandma's face. She lay back in her bed, closed her eyes, and passed away.

Louis Communicated Through EKG Machine

In the early 1980s, I was working with a young man named Louis, who was in a coma after being struck by lightning in Miami and almost died. He was flown to a hospital on Long Island where they were better equipped to help him. His body was twisted and arms bent. I could feel the agony just by looking at his face. He was connected to a myriad of medical machines including an EKG machine to monitor his heartbeat and a tracheotomy tube which helped him breathe. It was a miracle he survived the lightning strike. Without the life-support equipment he surely would have died.

We first learned about Louis through a newspaper article where his parents were pleading for help. The doctors had done everything they could; the family had nowhere to turn. I went to the hospital to meet with his parents along with my wife, Diana, and my spiritual mentor, Michelle. Louis's parents agreed to let us visit him and work with him.

We went there to use therapeutic touch — also known as the laying of hands — to send healing energy from the Creator through our hands into him. We don't actually touch the patient physically; we connect with the aura, which is an energy field surrounding the physical body. The laying of hands is an ancient healing process in which the healer becomes a conduit for divine healing energy which is transferred to the patient through the palms of the hands. This will strengthen their spiritual energy healing them on the seed level.

Doctors treat a branch of the tree with medicine; we also need to treat the seed of the tree spiritually and holistically.

We had to get clearance from the staff in order to spend time with Louis. The nurses who were working in ICU made no attempt to hide the fact they thought we were nuts. They were not rude but it was obvious that we were not welcome.

The first day we started sending healing energy to Louis. We came back to see him the next few days and repeated the procedure. There was no response but I didn't really expect one. On the fourth day I was sending healing energy to Louis through the palms of my hands around his chest and I asked him telepathically if he could hear me. As I did this, the EKG machine registered a skipped heartbeat. I asked him to answer some simple yes and no questions by regulating his heartbeat. I watched the waves on the monitor move a particular way. That was a yes. After a few moments I asked if he could see me; he answered yes.

After a short while I asked him for permission to work with him, and the EKG machine started fluctuating more than ever! That was a resounding yes! I was stunned! I was able to communicate with him through the EKG machine.

Just at that moment the nurse came running in yelling,

"What the hell are you doing in here?"

Taken aback, we assured her that everything was fine and she had nothing to worry about.

She said, "I don't know what you are doing here, but you better stop it."

A monitor at the nurses' station was hooked to the EKG machine and the nurses had seen the fluctuations in Louis' heartbeat.

I spoke to her outside for a few moments to calm her down and reassure her that everything was OK. I explained to her what I was doing; she never bothered us again.

I told Louis we would return the next day. I was so excited I could hardly eat dinner. He heard me! What a breakthrough. Diana and I were sitting in a booth looking over the menus when all of a sudden the spirit of Louis showed up. I told him to go back to the hospital, but he would have none of it. He wanted to be with us for a while; finally someone could hear him. It was very sad and frustrating for him to watch his family suffer. After dinner was over his energy faded.

The next day we took music to the hospital. "The Love Theme" from the movie Flashdance is a potent instrumental that sends powerful healing energy right to the soul. It still does today. I used therapeutic touch while playing that song over and over filling the room with healing energy. Louis loved it. He responded by manipulating his heartbeats.

His body was frozen in a contorted position for so long his muscles atrophied and he was rapidly deteriorating. He didn't want to return to his body and one night he broke free and went home. A while later Louis visited us in spirit to thank us and say good-bye.

People Hide Spiritual Experiences

Most people are afraid to talk about spiritual experiences like these; they are afraid people are going to think they are crazy. But these experiences are more common than most people realize. In an auditorium full of people almost everyone would raise their hand if asked if they had ever had a spiritual experience. It is time for our society to come out of the spiritual closet and start to share these profound experiences.

I meditate before I do any spiritual work in order to raise my vibrations high enough to make contact with spiritual beings that are lowering their vibrations low enough for us to exchange information. It's all about energy. Everything is energy.

The only difference between a medium and someone with Alzheimer's or dementia is that the medium comes back to the physical body where as an Alzheimer's patient moves forward into the spirit world and does not come back.

If we have a friend or relative with Alzheimer's in a nursing home, we need to be sure to include them in the birthdays, holidays, and weddings because they are there with us and our loved ones in spirit.

Prayer is the most powerful tool we have to help them move forward. It puts wind in their sails. It is important to remember that we have loved ones in the spirit world watching over them as well. It's comforting to know we are not alone.

When we see bad things happen to the people we love, it provides us with the opportunity to learn about unconditional love, compassion, sacrifice, charity, patience, and forgiveness here at the Earth School. If everything was perfect how would we learn priceless spiritual lessons?

> The intuitive mind is a sacred gift and the rational mind is a faithful servant. We have created a society that honors the servant and has forgotten the gift.
> ~Albert Einstein

Chapter 18

Suicide

Suicide is a permanent answer
to a temporary problem.
~unknown

There is an epidemic of suicides and attempted suicides in our country today. We live in a 24-7 world where most people are ill-equipped to handle the stress and anxiety this rapid pace generates.

Without a solid spiritual foundation some people turn to drugs and alcohol to escape. Some people are so desperate for change they break their life contract and go home early through suicide. Surprisingly a large number of suicides today are young people; some are only children.

Nationally, suicide is the third leading cause of death among young people fifteen to twenty-four years old. What is going on? How can life be so bad that a child would take their own life?

Those who commit suicide think they are powerless victims not realizing they have other options. Some of the desperate jumpers that have launched themselves from the Golden Gate Bridge in California miraculously survived the fall and were asked about the experience. Almost all of them realized halfway down they had made a horrible mistake by wanting to die and they did indeed have a lot to live for. Somehow they got a second chance. How many of those jumpers who died realized the same thing before they hit the water? Most of them probably had the same experience.

People who attempt suicide and do not succeed are left with the original problem and with the residual effects of the attempt. There are many reasons why someone would choose to commit suicide, ranging from having a painful terminal illness and not wanting to be a burden on the family, to losing all their money in the stock market or breaking up with a lover. Other suicides are victims of physical, emotional and/or mental abuse. The list goes on.

Ultimately suicide is a selfish act. The true victims are the family and friends they leave behind; their feelings of pain and guilt are overwhelming.

Suicide is *never* written into anyone's life chart. We are never given more than we can handle in life; it would cancel out the reasons we came here. Granted at times we are asked to endure overwhelming circumstances and seemingly insurmountable challenges but suicide or attempted suicide is never the answer.

Suicides are often avoidable tragedies. Most of the time there are warning signs, however they are either not recognized or ignored. When the lines of communication are severed these desperate souls are crying out for help.

Suicide Victims Do Not Burn in Hell

The question I am asked most often is, "Is my (loved one) burning in hell?" because the church tells us that those who commit suicide go to hell. That's like handing bricks to a drowning man. This cruel and ignorant teaching is another false belief with its roots in the dark ages. If humanity is going to survive, we need to unlearn what we were taught and relearn. People who commit suicide were already living in hell. That's why they killed themselves. Hell is not a place it is a state of mind.

Suicide victims do not go from hell to hell. When suicides go home to the Light they wake up and realize they broke their life contract at the very lesson they came here to learn. Life is a precious gift; it takes a tremendous amount of energy and effort to be born. Earth is a very tough school. We are in a combat zone of our own making here at the Earth School. Life can be heaven or hell depending on our level of awareness. Souls are always treated with unconditional love and compassion when they go home to the Light.

Hell is not an external place; it is internal. Fear, guilt, hatred, anger, resentment, jealousy, negativity are all by-products of hell. When we close ourselves off from the Light in consciousness, we see only darkness. Master teacher Jesus told us, "The Kingdom of Heaven is within you." Heaven is not an external place either; it too is

within us. Love, joy, peace, unity, happiness, forgiveness, and tranquility are all byproducts of Heaven. When
we open ourselves up to the Light in consciousness, there
is no darkness. We take the Light inside us wherever we
go, even after death.

> Hell is distance from God,
> Heaven is nearness to God...
> ~*Zohar*

Some souls do not return home to the Light. They
choose to stay here on Earth in the Astral Plane, the
fourth dimension, a place we go immediately after death.
They turn their backs on the Light, which is always
available to them for a number of reasons. Some souls
have an attachment to a particular place they lived or enjoyed. Alcoholics will hang around a bar while drug at-
tics will hang around a drug den trying to feed off the
energy to which they were addicted on Earth. Other souls
stay in the fourth dimension because they fear the wrath
of punishing tribunals at the final judgment they were
taught about in church. There are many other reasons
why a soul would not choose to go home to the Light.
None are valid, all are born of ignorance.

These souls are known as poltergeists or ghosts. Souls
that return home to the Light are Spirits. Eventually all
souls return home, but no one is ever forced into the
Light. Just remember, when we die, we shouldn't hang
around here. We should go straight home through the
tunnel of Light. We can always come back as a spirit to
visit our families and friends.

All suicides who return home to the Light are met by angels or beings of light expressing unlimited unconditional love and compassion. Angels take them to a tranquil place in isolation where they can unpack their bags of unfinished business and chaos. Here they are able to regain their balance and composure. Often they are in the company of animals, sometimes a beloved pet. Animals radiate unconditional love and have a calming effect that helps bring peace and tranquility.

After they regain composure, their Spirit Guide comes to get them to guide them through their life review. First the soul gets to see the life they would have had, had they not committed suicide. They realize there were other options they could have chosen and that they bailed at the very lesson they came here to learn. Then one by one they get to feel the emotional impact their suicide had on everyone they left behind.

I have done many readings where people who committed suicide came through. They are some of the hardest readings I have to do, especially when children are involved. All of them regretted their actions. Most of them never realized how deeply they were loved and how much energy their loved ones put into helping them keep their head above water.

The survivors of suicide victims have to cope with the emotional pain and guilt and often the false belief that their loved one is burning in hell. Suicide victims get to feel their loved ones grief and anguish, as they struggle to keep their heads above water. Who's in hell now?

After the returning soul goes through their life review, they are reunited with their soul group to rest, recharge and prepare for their next incarnation. As soon as the soul is ready it must return to school and face the same exact situation in their next life. Only this time it will be even harder. This provides another opportunity for the soul to learn the spiritual lesson it was avoiding in their last life. If they commit suicide once more the process starts all over again. There is no escape. Suicide is a waste of time.

We Come to Earth Fully Equipped

No one comes to earth without enough tools, powers, and abilities to learn their lessons because that would defeat the very reason we came here. Think about it.

Why would God, who is unconditional love, compassion, merciful and forgiving, condemn someone to hell for all eternity? Especially if they were in so much emotional and or physical pain that they broke their life contract? It doesn't make sense. If God knew we didn't have enough tools to overcome the challenges in life He would be creating people just to sentence them to eternal damnation. This would make God an absolute madman.

The big problem is people don't know who they really are. No one would commit suicide if they knew they were divine beings with unlimited potential. They would remember Earth is a school they *volunteered* to come to and they were born with profound spiritual powers and abilities. If people knew they would have to come back and face the same exact situation all over again in their next life, no one would break their life contract.

> The spiritual life does not re-
> move us from the world, but it
> leads us deeper into it.
> ~ *Henri Nouwen*

The high percentage of suicides among millionaires proves money can't buy happiness. Sometimes the money takes on a life of its own turning family members against each other. Many people work so hard building a successful business that their family life suffers. Spouses cheat, children do drugs, and business partners steal. Their material possessions no longer bring them happiness, contentment or fulfillment and they have no capacity to love. The final act of power and control is to take their life.

> The truly wealthy person is not
> the one who has the most. It is
> the one who needs the least.
> *~Interview with God*

The more we understand about the spirit world, the more we come face to face with our divinity. The spiritual path leads us to self-empowerment. When we are self-empowered we are able to make better choices and decisions. We replace chaos with fulfillment and pain with joy.

Problems we are experiencing today stem from erroneous religious doctrines stuck in the Middle Ages while the rest of the world is living in the twenty-first century. Religion must grow and evolve with the times. If the church, instead of the Wright Brothers, invented the airplane we would still be flying the same plane they flew at Kitty Hawk today.

The church does not change in a world that is constantly changing. The high rate of suicide and attempted suicide in the world today is because people do not have a solid spiritual foundation to stand on. These desperate souls forgot they are powerful spiritual beings with unlimited potential. Our spiritual powers and abilities are not nurtured, they are suppressed. We need to know who we are, where we are, why we are here, and how to use this vital self-empowering information to live rich and meaningful lives. Practical spirituality, which we can use in our everyday lives, is far more important than all the hallelujahs and amen's put together.

I'm not saying organized religion is bad; I am saying it is limiting. We need to move beyond the walls of fear, guilt and dogma to awaken to our true spiritual identity, our higher self. Remember, we are spiritual beings in human form and the higher self is our connection to the Divine Source. The path to awakening and self empowerment begins with one small step. It is our responsibility to take that step. Self-empowered people do not commit suicide, they help prevent it. The life we save may be our own.

> All learning is remembering, all
> teaching is reminding, all lessons are memories, recaptured.
> All knowledge is within.
> ~unknown

Chapter 19
Spirit Communication

Those who danced were
thought to be quite insane by
those who could not hear the
music.

~ Angela Monet

Spirit communication is a three-way process; it is a flow of energy from Spirit, through the medium to you. It's like water flowing through a hose. The more open you are to the spirit world the better the flow of energy will be. If there's someone in particular you are hoping will come through they probably will. However they may not be the first one through, so honor and respect whoever comes through first; that keeps the energy flowing.

I normally get a crowd during readings. Rarely do one or two people come through alone. Sometimes I can't distinguish between in-laws or ex-in-laws. A father in law will come through as a father and a stepfather will come through as a father as well. I also get people outside the family circle who can go all the way back to your childhood, a friend, neighbor, coworker or classmate.

There are times you may be asked to deliver messages because the spirits know when you're opening a phone line to the other side and they may ask you to pass messages to their loved ones. I am the medium for you and you are the medium for your family and friends, but you have to be careful when you deliver messages.

Going up and knocking on someone's door and telling them that you spoke to their departed mother last night might not go over big with a lot of people. If it doesn't feel like the right time, it's not. Trust your intuition; the spirits will provide a window of opportunity for you. It could be in three days or in three months. Intuitively you will know when the time is right.

Spirits, just like people do not all communicate equally. Some spirits are better communicators than others and are able to get my attention easier. Someone who has been on the other side for a long time is not necessarily a better communicator. In fact children are excellent communicators.

If you have a relative in spirit who never spoke English it could be a problem for me on this side, because I only speak English. However, the language barrier is resolved because of the way I receive information from the spirit world. I may have a hard time getting their name but I will always understand what they want me to say.

People can come through who you didn't know in life,

like a grandmother or grandfather that died before we were born, and people you did not like in life can come through as well. Nothing is going to stop them. There may be forgiveness issues which need to be addressed in order for these spirits to move forward.

I had a client who only wanted to speak to her mother when suddenly her Uncle Fred appeared. She hated Uncle Fred and told me to make him go away. I told her I couldn't do that until forgiveness issues were resolved with him. After those issues were addressed her mother came through. This is not McDonald's; you cannot say, "Give me Grandma, Grandpa, large fries and Coke." The spirit world is in charge of who comes through and in what order. If someone you do not like calls you on the telephone, you can't blame the phone. Mediums are a telephone to the other side. We give the spirits a voice.

You might not remember or recognize a name or initial right off the top of your head. Just write it down and put a question mark next to it. This keeps the energy flowing. I am not reading your mind and I can't expect you to be the family historian on the spot. Half the fun is finding out who those people are later on. For example, your deceased Grandmother may come through with a lady named Ruth. You have no idea who Ruth is at the time, only to find out later on she was your Grandmothers best friend.

If someone was called Bob or Bill and I give you the name Robert or William it's the same person. I usually get the name on the birth certificate. If I hear Robert and Bob, that means there are two Roberts. For the most part Spirits do not repeat the same thing unless there's more than one or you do not acknowledge that name. Spirits are persistent. Wouldn't you be persistent if someone did not recognize your name?

Clients Often Experience 'Psychic Amnesia'

During a reading you may get "psychic amnesia." You forget your mother's name, your sister's name or even your own child's name. The name Paul came up during a reading and the client didn't know who he was. I told her to write it down and put a question mark next to the name. The next day the client called and told me she just remembered her older brother's name was Paul but they always called him Skip.

I can't tell you how many times that happened. I used to let it drive me crazy until I learned later on the information I received was correct. That is why I tell you to write down the name and put a question mark next to it. Many times I get names, places, and events the client didn't know about until they ask other family members or check the family genealogy. This proves I am not reading your mind.

Sometimes information which was withheld from you for one reason or another in life is revealed by a loved one on the other side during a reading. If I receive information from the other side, you are supposed to know about it; I don't receive information that cannot be validated. Unless you know the family genealogy I will not get ancestors you cannot identify. I have had remarkable readings with families who knew their genealogy. Some of these readings were rich with history. There were many where soldiers who fought in the Civil War came through.

One time a soldier who fought in the Revolutionary war came through wearing a tri-corner hat and carrying a musket. He told me his full name and where he was from. A short time after the reading the family went to Massachusetts, located his grave, and paid their respects.

I don't see spirits as clearly as I see you and I don't hear them as clearly as I hear you. This is inter-dimensional communication, a language of energy.

I have an obligation to provide you with all the information I receive from the other side, the good, the bad and the ugly, even information about future events. When I receive information it's because you are supposed to know about it. The Spirits don't tell me everything, like the cure for cancer or the winning six Lotto numbers (believe me I've tried and it doesn't work) because that would be like going up to the teacher and saying, "Give me the answers to the test so I can get a perfect score."

Tuning in the Spirit World is Honed Skill

Mediums connect the physical world and the spirit world. Through meditation I am able to raise my energy frequency high enough to tune in spirits who lower their vibrations so we can communicate with each other.

The ability to communicate with spirits is honed over time like any other skill. If you want to be a concert pianist or a black belt in karate you practice the disciplines necessary to achieve those goals. Spirit communication is a discipline based in meditation. People who meditate regularly have the capacity to communicate with nonphysical beings because they are tuned in to the spirit world.

The process of spirit communication is actually very scientific. Cutting-edge discoveries in quantum physics point straight to the spirit world. (This is making the scientific community very uncomfortable.)

Do you need to know the laws of physics that operate a cell phone in order to use it? Of course not; all you need to know is how to turn it on and what buttons to push. Mediums are quantum cell phones. We don't need to know the laws of physics to communicate with spirits; all we need to know is how to turn it on and tune in.

Tuning in to the spirit world is like tuning in a radio station. Mediums create an opening in their minds for spirits to come through. This doorway to the other side is only found in the present moment, the Now.

Meditation opens the door. (Spirits also visit us in dreams because during sleep we are in the *Now* but that connection is on an unconscious level.) Once I open the door, spirits come through one at a time. The Spirits, not the mediums are in control. My Spirit Guide Thomas is the gatekeeper who watches over me from the other side.

I use *clairvoyance* (clear seeing), *clairaudience* (clear hearing), *clairsentience* (clear sensing), *clairalience* (clear smelling) and *claircognizance* (clear knowing) during my communications with the other side.

The following explains how each works.

➤ **Clairvoyance:** I see spiritual beings clairvoyantly as light energy in human form. Sometimes it's hard to make out facial features, but other times I see them so clearly I can count their eyelashes.

I see pictures, images, and symbols clearly. When I see a birthday cake I know it is someone's birthday. If I see a red cross on my client's chest I know they are in the medical field. If I see a desk with an apple on it I will know the person is a teacher. If I see a surgical incision with stitches, I will talk about a surgery. If it's a long incision with many stitches it's a serious surgery. I know where the operation is by where the incision and stitches are on the body. For example, if I see stitches running down the center of the chest I'll talk about heart surgery. I'm not a doctor so I do not diagnose anyone.

This is a Spirit's way of bringing attention to that area. They want you to know they are watching over you or another family member with a health issue. They will show me a series of symbols to provide specific information. It's like a game of psychic charades.

Spirits show me some of the craziest things. Sometimes I see hemorrhoids when the spirits are talking about someone being a pain in the butt. Yes, they do have a sense of humor. If someone was a comic on Earth you can bet they are still laughing on the other side. After all, what kind of place would Heaven be without fun and laughter?

One time I was reading a young lady who lost her boyfriend, Max, the previous year in a motorcycle accident. He came through and the first thing he did was give me the finger! I asked him, "What the heck am I supposed to do with that? Do you want me to give her the finger?"

I asked her if Max was a funny guy and she said yes.

I told her, "He'd better be because he's giving me the finger."

She started laughing and said that's how they always greeted each other. The hand signal was an endearing gesture between them. Go figure.

Another time a young girl's father came through holding a box of Dunkin' Donuts. At first I thought he worked there. When I looked closer at the box and he showed me they were the doughnut holes called Munchkins. I asked her, "Who is the Munchkin"?" She told me that her father always called her his little "Munchkin."

It's incredible to see how clever the spirits can be.

I had a reading with a woman named Roseanne who lost her daughter Toni to cancer. Roseanne was her caregiver. Toni came through in the reading and told her mother she needed to let go of some unfinished business; she was carrying around emotional baggage concerning Toni that wasn't hers.

As soon as I relayed that message, Roseanne became angry. "I have no unfinished business with my daughter!" she snapped as she leaned forward staring into my eyes.

Shaken, I turned to Toni and asked her to "please help me out here or your mother's going to kill me!"

Toni showed me a stack of pancakes.

"Pancakes? I'm supposed to talk about pancakes? If I tell her pancakes, she is going to nail me to the wall!" But intuitively I knew I had to tell her about the pancakes because the first rule of being a Medium is to *trust* the information you receive from the spirit world.

Cautiously, I told Roseanne that Toni was showing me a stack of pancakes.

As soon as I mentioned the pancakes Rosanne broke down and started crying. She went from one extreme to the other in a heartbeat. After a few minutes she calmed down and explained that one day she got home from work and cooked a chicken dinner for the family. Toni was very weak from all the chemotherapy so Roseanne brought dinner to her bed. When Toni saw the chicken she told her mother she wanted pancakes.

Roseanne was really stressed from everything that had been happening and lashed out at her daughter. "After working and doing chores all day, then making everyone dinner and now you want pancakes!" Roseanne stormed out of the room and made Toni pancakes. A short time later Toni died.

Roseanne has been carrying the guilt of getting angry about the pancakes the whole time. Rosanne said if she could get Toni back she would make pancakes for her every day. The pancakes were a *huge* message of forgiveness and love from her daughter.

Toni and the butterfly

Our loved ones on the other side can fuse their energy into simple life forms such as butterflies, dragonflies, ladybugs and birds in order to get our attention. They do this by having them to either land on us, or come up very close. For example, when Roseanne went to her daughter Toni's funeral service, her family released a bunch of butterflies during the ceremony. All the butterflies flew away except for one beautiful multicolored butterfly that landed on Roseanne's head and remained there throughout the entire service. Everyone's eyes were on this tiny little butterfly sitting on Roseanne's head gently flapping its wings back and forth as happy as could be. This amazing butterfly had the power to lift the energy in the entire room because everyone knew it was Toni. To this day people still talk about it. One of the first things Toni validated during her mother's reading was the butterfly event. The following year Roseanne lost another daughter to cancer and Toni was there to meet her sister Leeann.

Another amazing thing our loved ones in spirit can do is fuse their energy into a pet dog or cat in order to snuggle us. As spirits, they cannot feel the warmth of our physical bodies. So they (are able to) fuse their energy into a pet dog or cat in order to lie beside you and snuggle. Remember this the next time your pet is being extra affectionate.

➢ **Clairaudience:** Spirits communicate telepathically. I don't hear them with my ears, I hear them in my mind. It sounds much like when you're reading something silently to yourself; I've learned to separate their voices from my thoughts.

Sometimes the messages are clear as a bell and other times they sound like someone hanging out of a car window and yelling a name at me as they drive by doing sixty miles an hour. Spirit communication is a language of energy. We are human radios receiving thought signals from the spirit world.

People without spiritual beliefs during their lives come through the loudest. I had a spirit named Frank who pushed his way to the front of the line to contact his wife during a group reading. This powerful spirit pulled me to a woman sitting in the back of the room. I told her that her husband was here to speak to her and he gave me the name Frank.

"That's impossible, it can't be him."

"Why not, he's dead isn't he?"

"Yes, Frank died last year, but he didn't believe in any of this."

Trying not to laugh too hard I said, "He does now!"

Everyone becomes a believer when they die. Any skeptic who says they don't believe in any of this will find out differently when they die and come looking for a medium just as Frank did.

➤ **Clairsentience:** Part of the spirit communication process is feeling sensations on my body.

When I feel a pressure in the center of my chest I will talk about a heart attack. If I feel my throat close and my breathing become labored, I will talk about throat cancer, lung cancer or some other respiratory issue.

This is my least favorite way of receiving information, but it comes with being a medium. I'm not in pain but sometimes the sensations can be uncomfortable. Years ago when I began communicating with spirits, I had aches and pains all over my body. I thought I was getting old quickly. Then I began to notice after the reading was over I felt fine, no aches or pains. It took me a while to figure out these sensations were not mine and what they meant. They were messages from the other side.

As soon as I figured out their meanings, everything was fine. So when I feel a sensation I talk about that part of the body. I feel sensations in my kidneys, liver/pancreas and other organs as well. These sensations usually refer to health issues the spirit had but they can also be for people here they are watching over.

We are not facing health issues alone. We have the support of our families, friends, and loved ones on the other side. We are not the only ones in the hospital room. They are our invisible spiritual support team. It's nice to know our loved ones are still with us at such times.

➢ **Clairalience:** During a reading I may smell tobacco, alcohol, or another scent to receive information from the other side.

Alcohol is what I smell most frequently because there are so many alcohol-related readings. In fact ninety percent of my readings would be different if alcohol was never on the face of the Earth. That's how many people sign up for the alcohol class here at school.

I also smell flowers, perfume, and other pleasant fragrances. As a matter of fact, so do you. Your deceased grandmother might make you smell the aroma of her favorite perfume to let you know she's still watching over you. Or perhaps out of nowhere you may smell your father's favorite pipe tobacco. Your loved ones will often use the scent of flowers to let you know that you are not alone. Spirits are adept at utilizing familiar odors and fragrances to get your attention.

The problem is your logical reasoning mind is designed to separate you from these spiritual events. You may automatically think it was wishful thinking or a figment of your imagination. Don't let anyone or anything separate you from recognizing these signs from spirit. Next time this happens acknowledge your loved ones presence because he/she put a lot of effort into making these events happen. This is the spirits' way of letting you know they are still part of your life.

What would you do if you were on the other side trying to get someone's attention? That's exactly what your deceased loved ones are doing to you.

➢ **Claircognizance:** Spirits sometimes download information and I just know what they want me to talk about. For example there are times I'll know that someone had a farm in Pennsylvania and the barn burned down. I won't see it, hear it or feel it, I'll just know it.

This is my favorite way to receive information. It comes out of the blue so I have to recognize when it happens. I tell the spirits before we begin that I prefer receiving information this way. This works great when the information is positive, uplifting, and healing but when it is negative in nature I feel that too. If someone was physically abused I will be in the middle of it. Unfortunately I have often dealt with abuse issues.

This work is all about love and forgiveness but there is a dark side which needs to be respected, not feared. I protect myself before I open up to the spirit world and do any readings. Spiritual protection is explained in the next chapter.

You are a Medium, Too

Everyone is born with the same powers and abilities. It's just a matter of learning how to develop them. In the West we are taught not to use them because they are considered occult and the work of the devil. Nothing could be farther from the truth. Unfortunately many people are still stuck in the dark ages with this mindset because of their religious upbringing.

Your loved ones on the other side can hear you when you talk to them verbally or telepathically. They talk to you too. You need to learn how to listen.

Spiritual beings are electro-magnetic energy and they can interact with technology. They can make lights, televisions, computers, clocks, or any other electrical item turn on and off. They can make door bells and phones ring when no one is there. Some spirits have left messages on voicemail and others were able to text messages to their family. They can make songs play at key moments to remind you of them or point you in the right direction.

For example, if you are confused about something and looking for guidance, your deceased loved ones might give you the guidance you seek in the lyrics of a song that comes on the radio at a key moment. But you must have the ears to hear otherwise you will miss the message.

There may be times you are so worried about something you're not paying attention. You don't see the life preserver that just hit you in the head. Perhaps the guidance you seek will come on a billboard or a bumper sticker.

When you have the eyes to see and the ears to hear, you realize your family, friends, and loved ones on the other side are not just talking to you, they are shouting at you. The key is to learn how they communicate with you.

> Your talent is God's gift to you.
> What you do with it is your gift
> back to God.
> *~Leo Buscaglia*

Chapter 20
Spiritual Protection

What lies behind us and what lies
before us are small matters com-
pared to what lies within us.
~Ralph Waldo Emerson

Before you do any spiritual work, you need to protect yourself. Having a séance or playing with Ouija boards may sound like fun, but if you do not know how to protect yourself you are asking for trouble. Working with the spirit world without protection would be like having a party and letting anyone off the street in your home.

An earthbound ghost with negative energy could seize the opportunity to create a lot of fear, stress, and anxiety. A dark, negative energy could stay around you and your family and feed off your energy for awhile. Remember everything is energy and a ghost can attach itself to your energy to recharge. A ghost cannot hurt you but it has the potential to create a great deal of fear and anxiety. Life is challenging enough without an unwanted earthbound entity in your home.

One thing you can do is create a sacred space in your house. A small altar with a white tablecloth and some spiritual objects to keep the energy vibration high — a white candle, pictures, holy books or whatever you feel a spiritual connection with. This will help maintain positive and harmonious energy in your home.

Another form of protection is smudging — burning of sage or other herbs to purify people, homes, workspaces, and objects. The effect of the smoke is to banish negative energies that can bring physical, emotional, and spiritual imbalance. Many different cultures around the world use this practice in their sacred rituals. Even the Catholic Church smudges with incense during High Mass and other ceremonies to ward off negative energies.

Smudging is used by healers who fan the smoke over the person using a feather or their hand from the top of the head to the soles of the feet. Blowing the smoke is not encouraged because you could be blowing negative energy into the smoke.

The energy field of plants blends with ours to create balance; this clears any unhealthy and negative energy.

When smudging your home, do one room at a time. Open the windows and doors to let out any stale negative energy and allow in fresh harmonious energy. Fan the smoke into the corners repeating whatever prayers you feel comfortable with. Energy collects in the corners of the room the way dust collects. If you could see negative energy it would be a dark smoky fog. Go from corner to corner in a clockwise fashion. Do not forget to do the closets. Visualize or imagine Angels standing in all four corners facing the center of the room. Picture the room filling with a radiant, healing, Divine White Light. As you go from room to room, repeat a prayer of protection like this one out loud or silently.

> The light of God surrounds me.
> The love of God enfolds me.
> The power of God protects me.
> The presence of God watches
> over me. Wherever I am God is.
> ~ J.D. Freeman

Now the room is clean and clear; close the windows and doors and go to the next room.

This should be done on a regular basis, once or twice a month. Negative energy is like dirt. If someone is bringing mud into the house every day you have to clean more often.

You will notice a house being lighter and brighter without the dense, heavy, negative energy infecting it. This is especially important when you are moving into a new home. You never know who lived there before you and what negative energy or entities they may have left behind.

> Our lives are not determined by
> what happens to us but by how
> we react to what happens, not
> by what life brings to us, but by

the attitude we bring to life. A positive attitude causes a chain reaction of positive thoughts, events, and outcomes. It is a catalyst, a spark that creates extraordinary results.

~Anonymous

Chapter 21
Other Dimensions

> I would rather live in a world
> where my life is surrounded by
> mystery than live in a world so
> small that my mind could com-
> pletely comprehend it.
> ~*Harry Emerson Fosdick*

Where exactly are these other dimensions? Why can't we see them? Can they see *us*? Can they *hear* us?

To get a better idea of where the spirit world is in relation to the physical world, imagine you are sitting in front of a large white screen. There is an image of a man moving around on the screen. The man on the screen lives in a flat, two-dimensional world consisting of length and height. He can move left and right and up and down on the large flat screen. But this two-dimensional man has no concept of width because his world is flat. Length, height and width make up the third dimension. We can see him clearly because we are outside of the screen looking into it; the two dimensional man cannot see us because we are in the third dimension. We are invisible to him.

If we were to say something to the man on the screen, our voices would sound as though they came from inside of his head. He would have no idea where our voices came from. Our voices would appear as thoughts in his mind. We could call his name, and he would be looking up and down, left and right — all over the flat screen — searching in vain to find us even though we are sitting right in front of him. And so it is with the spirit world. All the other dimensions surround each other in a similar way. Spiritual beings in other dimensions can see and hear us clearly and they can communicate with us telepathically.

Mediums communicate with spirits telepathically. I hear the spirits' thoughts in my head, and I speak to the spirits with my thoughts. In the spirit world, all communication is telepathic. As a matter of fact, *all* human beings are telepathic. It's a skill that can be honed like any other skill. One day humans will use mental telepathy instead of audio sounds to communicate. We are constantly receiving and sending thoughts telepathically to each other whether we are aware of it or not. It is a matter of learning to use it properly and editing any negative thoughts we are receiving from the collective consciousness.

In fact, Spiritual beings in other dimensions are in constant communication with us. Remember we are multidimensional beings that coexist in the physical world and in the spirit world simultaneously.

With practice, anyone can learn how to shift their attention away from the material world and communicate with the spirit world. We communicate with the spirit world every time we pray. We listen to the spirit world through meditation.

Spirit and Water

The spirit world is to humans as water is to ice. Liquid, ice, and vapor are various forms of the same thing: H_2O. We are spiritual beings (vapor) occupying a physical body (ice). The spirit world is ocean (liquid).

Spiritual Gravity

Following is a simple example of the fundamental difference between the physical and the spirit worlds.

Imagine there are two books. The first one is a cookbook that weighs five pounds.

The second one is a thin booklet filled with spiritual wisdom that weighs five ounces.

The effect of gravity on the thick cookbook is greater than the effect of gravity on the thin booklet.

In the spirit world however, it's just the opposite: Spiritual information has a much greater weight than physical mass. Gravity in the spirit world relates to information in the same way that gravity relates to mass in the physical world.

In the spirit world, the thin booklet filled with sacred wisdom carries much more weight and has a much greater presence than the large cookbook.

All the acts of love, kindness, compassion, charity, forgiveness, and service to others carry a lot of weight in the spirit world. External power, fame and fortune in the physical world carry no weight whatsoever on the other side.

> And the end of all our explor-
> ing will be to arrive where we
> started and know the place for
> the first time.
> ~*T.S. Eliot*

Appendix

Frequently Asked Questions

> **Why aren't most people aware of spirits?**

Everything depends on the person's energy field. If a person resonates at the right frequency they can easily connect with nonphysical beings by tuning in to their vibration. Most people have a low vibration frequency which makes it difficult for them to make these connections. Anyone can raise their frequency and tune in to the spirit world through conscious living and practicing the spiritual disciplines explained in this book. Everyone has the potential to communicate with spirits, some better than others. Everyone can sing, but not everyone will get a recording contract. Some people are naturally tuned in to the spirit world more than others. Young children are good spirit communicators because they are fresh from the other side. Many times a deceased loved one will appear to a grandchild during the funeral. Children do not know death and are naturally open because they live in the present moment. As the years go by they are taught to shut down their psychic abilities and get in line with everyone else.

➢ What happens when we die?

The soul leaves the physical body and enters the Astral Plane. From there the soul is supposed to move into the tunnel of white light that appears and return home to the spirit world. Some souls turn away from the light and choose to stay here on Earth. These earthbound entities are known as ghosts. When you die be sure to go straight into Light and reunite with your family, friends, loved ones and pets. They will all be there waiting to welcome you home.

➢ Why do some people choose not go into the light?

Some Earthbound souls feel strong ties to the living and do not want to leave, while others may be, murderers, addicts, suicides, as well as others who could fall into this category. Not all ghosts are negative, some souls who die suddenly in accidents or some other traumatic event are sometimes confused and don't even know they are dead. The 1990 movie "Ghost" portrayed Patrick Swayze as a murder victim trying to contact his wife. Along the way he met up with an angry man in the subway who was pushed in front of a train. These are excellent examples of ghosts. Later on Patrick is in a hospital where he meets an old man waiting to take his wife home to the Light when she dies. He was a spirit.

Some souls fear a final judgment, with punishing tribunals. Other souls have a strong affinity for the life they just left. The king may want to stay with his castle. The captain might stay with his ship and the farmer with his land. The alcoholic may want to stay at the bar to feed off the energy of other alcoholics. The drug addict will stay at the drug den to feed off the energy of the addicts. Murders and some suicides may want to stay because they don't understand what is really going on. The mother may want to stay with her children. Our spirit guides will give us some extra time if we choose to stay a little longer. Eventually they will call us home. Ignorance is the key factor for a soul not wanting to return home.

We can always return as spirits to visit loved ones on Earth.

The spirit world uses a different clock than we do in the physical universe. Years on Earth could be merely seconds in the spirit world. That's why we have ghosts haunting castles for hundreds of years. These earthbound energies had an emotional attachment to the castle and decided to stay here for a little longer. Meanwhile five hundred years goes by on Earth.

➤ **Can you communicate with a spirit if they have been reincarnated?**

It is possible to talk to deceased loved ones even if they have reincarnated because the soul divides. We are multidimensional beings. We do not come to earth with all of our spiritual energy. Most of our spiritual energy is on the other side. This is our higher self which is our direct connection with God. We bring only a portion of our spiritual energy with us to earth. If we brought all of our spiritual energy we would not be able to use our free will. Do you know why? Because we would know all the right things to do. It would be like a college graduate taking a first-grade test. So we come to earth with just enough spiritual energy to create the illusion of separation from the spirit world and our past lives so we can use our free will to overcome challenges, learn our lessons and accomplish our spiritual goals. Another portion of our spiritual energy can occupy another body on earth simultaneously and live another life. Right now part of your spirit could be an old man in China or little girl in Spain. This process does not apply to people living in the same family because it does not provide enough diversity for the soul's growth and development.

Picture this:

Imagine that everyone on earth is a drop of water. At death we return home to "the ocean" of spirit. We are all one with each other in this spiritual ocean. At any time, that drop which is grandma or grandpa, mom or dad, can come out of the ocean to visit us, communicate with us, or guide us home when we cross over.

➤ What is the white light?

This is the Divine White Light of God. The Light is not God, the way sunlight is not the sun. White Light comes from God the way sunlight comes from the sun. Everything in creation is made of this Divine White Light. All the vibrant colors of a rainbow are contained in white light. All the loving, joyful and healing attributes of the Creator are found in this Divine White Light.

➤ Why do spirits appear to us in human form?

We can recognize them this way. We are a species of "Light Beings." If your grandmother came to you in her true form you would not recognize her. So she appears to you as you would remember her. These are called *Soul Prints*. Many times our loved ones come to greet us when we die to guide us back home. The closer we get to home, the more we transform into the spiritual beings we truly are. This is an awakening. We *wake up* when we return home and remember who we really are, and why we came here.

➢ Why don't spirits tell us the cure for cancer and other deadly diseases?

We are at school. It would be like going to the teacher and asking for the answers to the test. The cure for cancer exists; it is our job to bring it from the spirit world into the physical world. The cure for polio existed before Dr. J. Salk brought it into the physical world. The airplane existed before the Wright brothers brought it into the physical realm. The cures to cancer, AIDS, diabetes, and other deadly diseases are waiting for us to bring them into the physical universe.

➢ Why don't spirits help us prevent violent crimes?

We cannot be told what to do or what not to do because that would cancel out our free will. We have an invisible spiritual support team of Spirit Guides and Guardian Angels watching over us always. Many warning signs are given; either people don't recognize them or they ignore them. How we exercise our free will determines our destiny. Everything depends on overcoming fear and making better choices and decisions. There are no accidents or coincidences. When we return home we understand how this one tiny fragment of a lifetime fits into a much bigger picture.

> **What is the difference between the soul and the spirit?**

The soul is part of the spirit that occupies the physical body. The spirit cannot occupy the physical body because it has a high-energy frequency. The soul is part of the spirit that is able to merge with the body on the sub-atomic level. After death the soul returns home to merge with spirit in the Light. Spirit, our higher self, is our truest essence and most perfect form.

For more information about the spirit world, including my calendar of events, appearances, seminars and workshops, please visit...

AlanArcieri.com

You will find a list of inspirational books and movies
I highly recommend on my website,
as well as links to other wonderful websites that
will help you continue your spiritual journey
on the path to awakening.
Namaste'

Printed in the United States
123454LV00014B/84/P